A New Identity Transformed by Truth

PHOEBE CRUISE

WestBow
PRESS
A DIVISION OF THOMAS NELSON

ISBN: 978-1-4497-7566-7 (sc)
ISBN: 978-1-4497-7564-3 (e)
ISBN: 978-1-4497-7565-0 (hc)

Library of Congress Control Number: 2012921420

WestBow Press books may be ordered through booksellers or by contacting:

WestBow Press
A Division of Thomas Nelson
1663 Liberty Drive
Bloomington, IN 47403
www.westbowpress.com
1-(866) 928-1240

Printed in the United States of America

WestBow Press rev. date: 11/19/2012

Acknowledgment

I want to give thanks to the Trinity: Father, Son, and Holy Ghost.

Dedication

This book is dedicated to all those who have lost hope in this world.

Contents

Prologue

My journey with our Lord Jesus Christ started when I was very young. I was attending a Catholic church, and at that time I didn't understand the whole gamut of Christianity, but I understood that God loved me. Even through all the challenges—parents' divorce, molestation, and other difficulties—I always knew that God loved me.

What I remember most about my childhood was that whenever I entered our church I felt cleaned and loved. And when the church rejected my family after my parents' divorce, I remember still wanting to go to church on my own. I was able to walk to church because we lived blocks away. It wasn't the building or people that brought me to church; it was this feeling of being cleaned and loved, and I knew that love emanating all around was God.

When I turned ten my mom received another job so my family moved to a new location. Because of the move, I was not able to walk to church so I didn't attend for a long time. I only thought of God when someone was in the hospital or died – and on certain holidays. When I moved out of the house and started college, I started talking to God on and off. Around this time I met my husband and we talked about having a large family. It was not until I had my firstborn that I felt I was missing something, or maybe missing out on something.

When I held my firstborn I remember feeling pure love for her and how wonderful it was to create a beautiful being out of love. That's when it hit me how much God loves us all. This unconditional love I had towards my newborn was just a fraction of the unconditional love God has towards us. In that moment I wanted to know God personally. I wanted my whole family to know God on a personal level, so we started attending church.

I accepted Jesus as my Lord and Savior in 1990, and suddenly my life took on a new meaning. I felt enveloped by the Holy Spirit. Prior to this I never understood the Holy Spirit's role, so I was confused when I started getting dreams, visions, and knowledge from the Lord. I wanted to know why I was getting these dreams, visions, and messages, and what it all meant. When I went to church the pastor was preaching on Paul from the New Testament or Jesus Christ. He never mentioned the Holy Spirit, yet here was something I desired to learn so I started reading the Bible and asking God to help me understand what I was reading. I still did not understand why I was getting these dreams, visions, and messages.

I would compare the pastor's teaching/interpretation to what I was reading in the Bible, and I remember being very confused. I asked God to help me in my confusion and to give me Truth. Filled with questions, I started writing to my pastor with my concerns. It seemed he often preached about God's *conditional* love—how a Christian should behave. I felt coerced to act a certain way and behave a certain way. I never understood how God could love us with conditions. I wanted to know God more so I kept reading the Bible. The more I read, the more a single thought took shape in my mind: *the God that I am reading about in the Bible is not the same God this pastor is preaching about.*

This particular church yielded to its political views because every teaching/preaching was prompted from a political stance. One Sunday during the election season, the church leaders gave the congregation a pamphlet regarding a certain political party and why the congregation should choose that party. I remember thinking *this has nothing to do with the Triune God*, and I felt as if I couldn't make any decisions on my own. Every time I went to this church I felt indoctrinated with lies. The pastor's teaching was so skewed on so many different levels, and I had to ask God for truth with every teaching given.

Spurred by my own frustration, I asked the Holy Spirit to help me move God's truth to people through Jesus Christ our Lord. I felt an urgency to write to this pastor about the truth I was receiving from God, but to no avail—he ignored me. So I decided to quit writing to him. Stung by his rejection, I didn't want God in my life anymore. Why was He giving me dreams, visions, and messages in order to speak truth into people's lives when it only fell on deaf ears? I asked God to help me understand why I had to go through this suffering when I felt rejected by people on so many levels. But I kept thinking about who is in control of my life: God or man?

With that question in mind I kept reaching for God and reading the Bible more. As I lay in bed one night I turned on the television to find Pastor Joel Osteen preaching (this was in 1999). His message was about "keeping on" and how if God put something in your heart you should keep the faith because He will be faithful to complete it. His message of encouragement resonated in my spirit. After receiving this encouragement I started progressing again. I wanted to know everything I could about God so I attended a Bible college to learn, grow, and earn a degree.

One of the professors from this school was a pastor from Woodland Hills Church in St. Paul, Minnesota, so I started attending this church. The more I desired to receive God's Truth, the more the Holy Spirit was activating in my life, giving me dreams, visions, and knowledge. I continually received certain scriptures to read and meditate on because God wanted me to keep His Word in my heart.

In early 2002 the Holy Spirit prompted me to give a message to this pastor/professor about his father: I needed to let him know that his dad had one good year left. This pastor is Greg Boyd and his father is Ed Boyd, and together they wrote the book *Letter from a Skeptic*. I had no intention to do anything else but bring forth this message to Greg about his father.

When I met with Greg to let him know what the Holy Spirit laid on my heart, his response was: "I don't understand; he is in good health…well, is it his heart?" I told him that I could not answer that. All I was supposed to do was deliver the message. At the end of the year, in December 2002, Ed Boyd passed away—that was just the beginning of my journey. It was in 2003 that the Holy Spirit prompted me to send my journal entries to Greg Boyd through email. I started emailing these messages and certain scriptures to Greg and Paul Eddy from the same church that year and continued until 2009. I decided to quit writing because I felt my messages were falling on deaf ears again.

Even though I felt discouraged because I wasn't receiving any response from the pastor, I received encouragement from the sisters in my prayer group. I decided to just commit to a deeper relationship with the Lord. Three years later, in 2012, I felt a nudging from the Holy Spirit to write again and send my dreams, messages, and visions to another pastor, Bill Bohline from Hosanna! Church in Lakeville, Minnesota. I also understood that it was time to get these writings in a book.

This book is a witness to the transformation of life to a new creation in Christ. I now have an urgency to get these messages to the public so that many will come to know the Lord and become a new creation in Him. This book is a personal spiritual journey for truth. God wants us to have a relationship with Him, and He wants us to understand how. All truth comes from one source: God, through His Word/Son, Jesus Christ, and His Holy Spirit.

Then you will know the truth, and the truth will set you free.

John 8:32 (NIV)

Letters to a Pastor

Hi Greg,

When the Lord came to me years ago and told me that He was going to make me an example to His church, I had no idea what that meant. But He planted a seed and I believed. I still don't know where all this is going, but I trust that He is in control. Yes, I have made mistakes along the way but He is always there to make good out of my bad choices.

I remember having these dreams and visions years ago and not knowing what to do with them, so I decided to write to my previous pastor to get some answers. Truth kept coming to my mind, and it differentiated from what I was hearing from the pulpit, but not the Bible. I wrote to this pastor because I wanted him to know what I was receiving and to get some feedback, but I rarely received a response.

When the Lord planted a seed in my heart about becoming a counselor, I was so excited I wanted to talk to the pastor about it. He only encouraged me to remain in the place where I was, and that was in the nursery. (When a church only acknowledges men in their roles and never encourages women in their gifting, it's time to move on.) I knew that what I was receiving was real and truthful, but whenever I entered this church I felt like I was in a vortex being sucked back into this world system of what we call life.

This went on for years and I couldn't take it emotionally anymore. I was becoming weaker and weaker spiritually so I asked the Lord to remove me from this church and connect me to a church that could explain what was happening to me. The Lord kept planting seeds, but it seemed as if I was getting nowhere and all I wanted to do was what the Lord planted in my heart—no one was going to rob, kill, or destroy this seed He planted.

I was crying most nights when the Lord spoke to me and gave me permission to leave this church and move on to another. I remember talking to a friend who encouraged my visions and dreams. That solidified my understanding and gave me hope. Her support encouraged me to go on. And then there was meeting you, which helped tremendously—now I could move forward.

The Lord told me that He is the giver of gifts and He can choose to do whatever He pleases with the gifts He has for each individual according to His will and purpose. God does not put limits on the gifts He has given. Man chooses to put conditions on God. When a person puts conditions on God it describes his or her picture of God, which tells me that he or she really doesn't know Him yet. If He wants me to speak, well, I am going to speak. If He wants me to do whatever He has for His will and purpose, I am going to proceed. I will not put conditions on the Lord; this only stifles the work of the Holy Spirit. I will not come against what the Lord has for me, and I will forbid anyone else to either.

Again, Jesus served with humility. Pride comes when the truth (Scripture) gets twisted. When one grows up in Christ he or she will let the Holy Spirit testify to the truth, and anything that comes against that is pure flesh or something else. I will not let the enemy penetrate this circle; I will shut that door. The Lord has given me a gift of discernment, and I can discern when a person operates from the flesh versus the Holy Spirit because I am under His authority and not man. When a person beholds His glory or beauty, they see with spiritual eyes. God is the righteous judge and His judgment is perfect. Condemnation is not of God. In Christ, transformation happens when love softens the heart. It is

His love that has a transforming power. It's so beautiful to be free of any criticism. The Lord is doing a beautiful thing in all those who believe in Him.

The key to faith is the belief that the Lord has our best interest at heart at all times. He is always for us and Satan is always against us. God wants us to be continually transformed. Just to let you know, I am never alone – God is always working, and He has surrounded me with so many sincere, imperfect Christians who have the heart of Christ.

The Lord gave me these Scriptures: 1 Corinthians 14, Mark 4, and Romans 10. He also told me to be careful of those who are legalistic because they are walking in pride. I pray that more preachers will know and attain the heart of Christ. How do we know when this will happen? Attainment will be reached when one has a personal relationship with the Lord, and when His body starts working together in a healthy way.

In Him,
Phoebe

Hi Greg,

When the Holy Spirit first started working in my life it wasn't easy. I was like a child learning about God in a new truthful way. I had to let go and listen and obey Him. The first year was all about learning truths and being obedient. I was given so many truths along with so many small assignments, and this still remains today. I am on a journey with the Lord, and I want to learn more about His truth. Jesus suffered, died, and was buried—but it did not end there. He rose again. And now He is working in the hearts of people bringing salvation to the world.

I was told many years ago that people would try to label me or accuse me of being something other than a disciple of Christ. Jesus told me they would have a hard time trying to fit me into another mold, but many will try and many will fail. He told me not to worry about what people accuse me of—their accusations stem from unbelief. He said, "Phoebe, if a person rejects you they are really rejecting Me."

The Lord showed me three crosses, and I heard: "One accepted, the other rejected – in these days there will be many scoffers and many will misunderstand you – take heart for I am with you always, even to the ends of the earth. Pray and love those who persecute you. I want all people to come into repentance and know Me more. I want no one to perish."

Jesus is so kind, gentle, loving, and wise. The Lord can do what He wants, when He wants, whatever He wants; He is the God of possibilities. Who are we to judge the Lord? I always have to remember that when we are in God's will we should let no one dissuade us from our Lord's doing. If people try we should do what Jesus did and say, "Get behind me, Satan." Remember this: we don't have to be the wisest, Jesus is. We don't have to be the most intelligent, Jesus is. We don't have to be the best tactician, Jesus is. We don't have to be the best strategist, Jesus is.

This week was a very emotional time. Earlier I had to bring one of my friends to the hospital, but I thought it was just preliminary. On Wednesday I woke up around 1 a.m. and my friend was on my heart. I heard in my spirit, "She is dying." I started to pray for her, and then I heard, "Pray for her family." I proceeded to pray for her family. I was praying for a miracle to take place and that God would heal my friend; I prayed for protection for her and her family as well as peace through all of this. As I was praying I heard, "Let her go." I had a hard time with this but I continued to pray and eventually fell asleep. I woke up and again prayed for a healing miracle, and again I heard, "Let go."

I really didn't know what was going on at the hospital so I called her room, and her daughter answered. She told me that her mom wasn't doing well and took a turn for the worse, and this morning she asked the doctor to let her die. My friend's daughter told me that her speech was getting worse, but her mom expressed her wishes. My friend's daughter said that now it is just a matter of time, and she outlined her plans for a Christian burial. I explained my messages to her, and she said that was about the same time she went off the road and over a ditch. She said it felt as if the car was going to flip over, but instead it turned and backed down the hill. She told me that she was fine and the car was fine. All she remembers is screaming "O Lord, help me!" She thanked me for praying, and I told her that I would continue to pray for her mom.

On Thursday when I got to the hospital room, my friend's daughter said her mom was no longer communicating and had been sleeping all day. Again I prayed in my heart for a miracle, and I moved face-to-face with my friend and told her I was praying for a miracle. She opened her eyes and said "I love you," and then she clearly said, "Please let me go." I stopped praying for a healing miracle and started thanking God for letting me know her. The Lord told me that she would be with Him in two weeks. And sure enough, two weeks later my friend was with God.

Death is just letting go of the physical body and lifting the spirit up to our Lord. She belongs to Him. May the God of love, peace, and joy be with you always.

Acts 13, Ephesians 4, Acts 14, Revelations 21

God bless you and Merry Christmas!

In Christ,
Phoebe

Hi Greg,

I started this journey with our Lord because of one very good reason – I wasn't getting the truth from the pulpit. Because of this, I went straight to God with questions and a yearning for truth. The idea that we should talk to people about hell before we speak about the truth of Christ is not only wrong, it has the wrong motivation (scare them out of hell). I brought this to our Lord and He said that in the grand scheme of things when people speak forcefully about hell it makes more people walk away from Him than engage with Him. It is wrong when pastors speak without seeking God first. This is a prime example of why I started my quest for truth.

Sadly, there isn't a lot of difference between a person in the political arena and a person speaking from the pulpit. This journey has put me in a position of bringing truth, waking up His church, and praying for all of God's people to engage with Him. I want to see more people brought into a relationship with God so they can see truth in the midst of darkness. We do not have any guarantees in this world but only one, and that is living our life eternally with our Lord after we take Him into our heart. This is why we need to press on with the truth about who He is and not smear His name.

You may bring facts to the pulpit, but remember to first speak truth – after seeking it. Truth always prevails. Whatever choices you make defines the path you are on. I choose Christ!

John 9, Acts 24, 4:11-12

In Him,
Phoebe

Hi Paul,

As I ponder today's message at church, I have only one thing to conclude: whatever the world assumes doesn't change the fact of what I know and what I believe. What I know and believe is that God "uses me" to change the world one heart at a time. What I see is a lost, hurting, suffering world that needs a Savior. I pray that God will use me effectively in any way to reach the world for Christ. Whether He uses me in the church or outside the church, I don't care—it's for God to choose. I am only answering the call He laid on my heart: John 17.

I pray that the body of Christ will come together by God's unified love. The body of Christ represents the family of God, and as one member of the body I will do whatever is in my heart not to let anything divide this body. This is also the same with the earthly family that God blessed me with. I will not let anyone or anything in this world divide us. A family signifies God's love and unity.

Our acts of love, faith, and obedience in Christ can make a difference in this world. Choose life in Christ and live! The world needs to know who Christ is and who they can become in Him. 1 John 4:16 (NIV): "And so we know and rely on the love God has for us. God is love. Whoever lives in love lives in God, and God in them."

In God's love,
Phoebe

Hi Greg,

I had a dream two weeks ago, and in this dream a snake came up to my face and showed me his fangs. The snake bit my arm and I felt the poison penetrating, but nothing happened – then I awoke. I asked God what this dream meant but I received no answer. I asked many people and received many different answers, yet nothing resonated within. Finally I heard in my spirit "Acts." After reading the book of Acts my answer resonated: Acts 28:5 (NIV): "But Paul shook the snake off into the fire and suffered no ill effects." Next I was told to read Isaiah and I kept hearing "The battle is the Lord's" and also "anarchy."

I had another unusual dream, and in this dream I became a woman of the streets, so to speak. Nothing happened to me physically, only emotionally. I remember being trapped emotionally and having feelings of helplessness, loneliness, and desperation. I kept saying, "There is no way out." I don't know what I need to do, but I will wait. I just wanted to let you know that my heart is for the people who, according to the world, are "the least of these." Everyone matters to the Lord, and they matter to me.

As I was praying Sunday morning I heard "What do you want?" My response was, "More of You and less of me." I want people to see Jesus in me so they will know that He is alive and real; this is my prayer. During another time in prayer I heard the following message from the Holy Spirit, and I think it is for you and many others in the church: "Leaders of the church obey My command to love one another just as I have loved you." I would love to give you anything I receive from the Lord if you will allow me to do so, and if not you need to let me know because I don't want to overstep my boundaries.

1 John 5, Romans 15

Peace,
Phoebe

Hi Greg,

Jesus is love: always has been and always will be. I hope and pray that one day soon we can all live together as a family, either black or white, male or female, Jew or Gentile—when all can truly feel our Father's love, which binds us together. I continually talk with my Father, day or night, rain or shine, in my car or in my house. He is my means of support, and I could do nothing without Him. My prayer is that you will bring light (truth) to as many people as God leads. Have a great Easter. I will be praying you through.

Peter 1:7

In truth,
Phoebe

Hi Paul,

I want to thank you for your time, and I appreciate your prayers. There were two scriptures that came to me before and after our meeting: 1 John 3:16 before and Matthew 18 after.

Relevant questions keep coming to mind as I ponder who we are in Christ. But it is not who we are but who we become. "Whatever is true, whatever is honorable, whatever is right..." – believe in this: Jesus Christ.

Why is it that all psychological reasoning comes down to two questions that explain our humanistic behavior: is it nurture or nature? Why there isn't another component called spirituality is beyond me. What component does God play in all of this? Nurture is of course genetics, which is how we are defined as a result from evolution (according to the researchers). And then you have nature, which defines our character from the world's perspective. With these questions in mind it presupposes that our predisposition does not identify with our Creator. Why do our researchers define all humanistic behaviors and set a norm for life? Researchers cannot define the supernatural, and I know that it sets a path to our thinking. All of our thinking becomes minimized. We need to break out of the natural and become who God created us to be in the supernatural. We need to defy all odds and become the body of Christ and be united as one.

In regards to the cognitive dissonance that we so often have it is because we are not rooted in Christ and we have too many choices that do not line up with God. Unchain the brain. Have the mind of Christ.

Philippians 1:6 (NIV): "He who began a good work in you is faithful to complete it."

Philippians 2:3 (NIV): "Do nothing out of selfish ambition or vain conceit. Rather, in humility value others above yourselves…"

In God's love,
Phoebe

Hi Paul,

I asked God, "How exactly does one become holy?" And He responded with this: "Sanctification; holiness is simplicity in its highest form and enjoying it." Simplicity does not mean poverty it just means that one should not be attached to this world. A prime example of this is Mother Teresa. I don't have to be doing; I just have to "be" before the Lord; therefore God will open the door to all eternity.

1 Peter 1:14-16 (NIV): "As obedient children, do not conform to the evil desires you had when you lived in ignorance. But just as he who called you is holy, so be holy in all you do; for it is written: 'Be holy, because I am holy.'"

Bless you,
Phoebe

Hi Greg,

Life is very exciting as it is wonderful to see God working in each heart. I often wonder how God could love me after all of my many shortcomings and wrong choices. All I know is that I am in God's light and He directed me there. And when accusation and condemnation come my way (from myself and others) I just rise above the pit and rest in Jesus' arms; I rest in His truth. It's hard to walk in love all the time, but we have a wonderful merciful God who knows our heart and can forgive us on the spot and love us anyway. How joyous and loving is that? I hope to live to see the day when all Christian sisters and brothers are united despite race, creed, or religion; this is my prayer.

St. Teresa: "Someone may come along one day and destroy what you have been building for years, but keep building. People will persecute and accuse you of wrongdoing, but love them anyway."

Philippians 4:13 (NIV): "For I can do everything through Christ, who gives me strength."

Colossians 3:14 (NIV): "And over all these virtues put on love, which binds them all together in perfect unity."

1 Corinthians 1:10 (NIV): "I appeal to you, brothers and sisters, in the name of our Lord Jesus Christ, that all of you agree with one another in what you say and that there be no divisions among you, but that you be perfectly united in mind and thought."

Be blessed,
Phoebe

―――――◦ఈ❀ఈ◦―――――

Hi Greg,

I pray that all of us will partner together with one focus and that is to love one another. What God did on the cross was not only to save our souls, and save humanity from destruction, but also to show His love towards humanity. God wants no one to perish, and He will go to great lengths to save humanity. This is why He sent His Son, so that the world will know God's love. In regards to John 17, if Christians would come together with this one focus, the focus to love without any conditions so that the world will know God by His love that was poured out on the cross by His Son, it could change the hearts of many all over the world. This love from God through His Son is the greatest story ever told.

I have a brother who worships Buddha; my love for him has never changed. I have a cousin who is gay, and my love for him is immense. I don't push religion; I am who God created me to be and that is to love without judgments.

I work with people who are poor, oppressed, homeless, blind, paralyzed, mentally unstable, and even dying from AIDS and Hepatitis B. Does this stop me from loving them? No, I love them more.

My heart also is to stand by people who are being attacked and lift them up. I don't care who you are or what you did; everyone deserves to be loved. I pray that the world will know God by His love! The scripture 1 Corinthians 13:4-5 came to me this morning which states: "Love is patient, love is kind. It does not envy, it does not boast, it is not proud, it does not dishonor others, it is not self-seeking, it is not easily angered, it keeps no record of wrongs."

Merry Christmas,
Phoebe

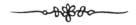

Hi Greg,

I received a message from our Lord that pertains to the church (Psalm 27 and Jude). Consider persecution as confirmation and just keep the faith and remain in love. I also received this message Wednesday morning: "Stay within the confines of marriage" and "You are a bride of Mine." Later I heard "Keep building." That same day I asked the Lord this question: "What can I do for You?" His answer: "Build My church." So many people are blinded to the truth that I am willing to do whatever it takes to open their eyes and open their hearts. I just want people to unite within the confines of His love; this is matrimony and we are His bride. Ezekiel 18: the Lord wants no one to perish.

Whatever they cannot see they cannot understand; whatever they cannot understand they cannot see.

In Him,
Phoebe

Hi Greg,

I told God that if He blessed me with children I would raise them according to His ways. And after each birth I dedicated each child to Him and asked God to help me raise these children. As a young mother I needed His help many times, and so many times I have seen His miracles take place. I remember the first time I heard His distinct voice…I was a young mother of two and I took my kids to a park for a children's festival with my brother. At the festival my son was getting fussy so I took him out of the stroller, and when I turned around my daughter, who was two at that time, had disappeared. There were about five hundred people at this festival, and she just vanished. Anxiety set in and I started to hyperventilate; all I could do was pray while I was in search for my daughter. We frantically searched everywhere. I remember having a hard time breathing, but I prayed and asked God for help—all I heard between the confusion was "stay."

All of a sudden I felt peace that filled my whole being, and I didn't move for a while. After about three minutes I had a hard time staying still so I started searching for her, and again I heard "stay." Once again, peace overwhelmed me. Out of nowhere this woman had Shandell on her shoulders, and it was the strangest thing—she walked right towards me. As she handed my daughter to me she didn't say a word and then she walked off. I knew this was an act of God.

There are so many times that God has helped me. When my youngest daughter was turning one she fell ill, and while I was taking her to the hospital her eyes rolled back into her head. Again I cried out to God for help and again I heard His voice: "She is going to be all right." After I heard His voice peace overwhelmed my soul. During the hospitalization the doctors were doing many tests to determine the cause of her illness, and the specialist didn't know if she was going to make it, but I remembered what God said and I was at peace throughout the whole process.

When my son pierced his hand with a nail, the nail didn't hit any vessels or tendons and today his hand is working 100 percent. And just last week the Lord told me that my daughter's welfare is more important than the car. The Lord has helped me so many times that I have become dependent on Him because I trust Him, and I don't want to go through life without God's guidance and help. I don't see how anyone can raise children without God's help or even go through life without our Lord's wisdom. Now do you see how this relationship developed? I trust God with all my heart, soul, mind, and strength.

Do you know what you get when someone preaches from the pulpit without the help of the Holy Spirit? You get a person speaking from the flesh. When one claim to know the Bible yet twists the Scriptures to fit his or her political view it displays nothing more than a person walking in the flesh. When one knows the Lord it is because of the Holy Spirit. He indwells all those who believe, but again many don't recognize the presence of the Holy Spirit because when one recognizes the Holy Spirit he or she no longer speaks from his own authority but with the Lord's authority. When one recognizes the Holy Spirit working he or she will be transformed.

How can a person have a personal relationship with God without the Holy Spirit? One needs to recognize the work of the Holy Spirit because without help from the Holy Spirit one can easily be deceived. I used to attend a church that did not recognize the power of God. God can use as many as ten thousand people or He may choose to use just one. We both know biblical history, and God can use one person to do His will if He so chooses. God gave people dreams and visions historically and He still does in the present— God is the same yesterday, today, and forever! Acts 2 says the Lord pours out His Spirit with dreams and visions, and when a person speaks from the pulpit and does not validate Scripture accordingly, this preacher just becomes a man talking with his own authority.

Do you know what will happen when one listens to a preacher who is operating from the flesh? It will lead to sin. It is imperative for preachers to let the Holy Spirit guide them because the Holy Spirit is truth and man can twist His Truth. Whenever I listen to a pastor who creates doubt in my mind, I go before the Lord and seek Truth. The Lord told me to let all those who don't believe fall by the wayside, and He reminds me to stay on the path set before me. I may not know where I am going but I do know where I will end up. The Lord told me to give these warnings to the ones who are creating doubt: "Take heed lest you fall" and "If anyone causes one of these little ones who believes in Me to sin, it would be better for him to have a large millstone hung around his neck and be drowned in the depths of the sea."

I can distinguish those who have a personal relationship with the Lord from those who just have head knowledge of Him. Many people may sound like they are speaking truth but they don't have the heart of God. The Lord told me that too many preachers preach with an unbelieving heart. The Lord told me the reason I am where I am is because I believe. I know that many preachers who are evangelical do not express the need to use the full gifting of God (cessation doctrine). But then they are not operating the full use of God's gifting.

We are finite human beings who are working with an infinite God. Let Him work in our hearts as He sees fit. The important thing is that we are coming under His authority and doing His will. I refuse to let anyone interfere with my relationship with God. I come under His authority. Now I see why He doesn't want me under man's authority. Seek His truth first.

One more thing I would like to add is that His law is in our hearts, and we are not under the law of lawlessness, which leads to religious tyranny – we are under the law of righteousness, which is under God. We need His laws because He is just and right, and when we mesh the laws of the world with His laws we get a bunch of people who think they are doing justice for the Lord when really it is just moral relativism. Moral relativism is justified by those who think they know the Lord and His ways, but they forget His first commandment: "Love the Lord God with all of your heart and with all of your soul and with all of your mind and with all of your strength…and love your neighbor as yourself." Know the Lord who sets you free from the law of lawlessness and who will set your mind on the things from above. There is power in His Word. Let His Word become your word, and claim it in Jesus' name. Amen!

James 3:9, James 3, Hebrew 2, 2 Peter 1, John 16, Luke 1:45

In Jesus' name,
Phoebe

Hi Greg,

The other week I heard: "Phoebe, walk humbly with your Lord, for you will face many challenges ahead." Also I heard: "I am your Lord and you are My people." I received 1 Corinthians 12 and 15. And just the other day I received Jeremiah 24, which ties into all the above. Another vision/dream I keep having is an eagle spreading her wings and flying high above, which to me exemplifies freedom and strength. Remember that whatever we do we do it for love because love never fails—nothing we do is in vain. There is a cross waiting ahead for all of us; we just need each other to get there.

Peace, love, and unity,
Phoebe

Hi Greg,

We both know that life has its ups and down. I asked this question of our Lord: "Why do we have to go through so much suffering before You return?" His reply: "It is through this suffering that unity and division are created." Unity is for Christ and division is for those who are against Him. There are too many confusing elements that contribute to the uncertainty of Christ. Many people are confused, and therefore we must stand firm and be a witness even if it is through suffering – it's vital that we stand as one.

Romans 11, 2 Corinthians 4, Isaiah 32

In Him,
Phoebe

Hi Greg,

I just had another dream concerning the end times. This dream was so real and so vivid. In this dream I was alone, and it was so dark and awful, but I knew what I had to do. Something inside inspired me not to be afraid. In this dream I kept leading people to Christ.

When I awoke the Lord asked me this question: "Why do you exist?" My response: "I exist to become more like You and to save souls for You." His response: "You have the holy spectrum inside you." He also told me that He created balance in my life and to let Him lead. I taught a class at Love Lines last night, and the words I spoke were words I needed to hear myself. "No matter what the situation is, always let the Lord lead your life – trust Him with everything He has given you." These are the Scriptures that came to me during the beginning of the week: Luke 9 (four times) and Psalm 29.

There are three passages of Scripture I received from the beginning that will never leave my heart: John 17, 1 Peter 1, and Ezekiel 33 (I am also to reflect on Ephesians 5 every day.) As much as I would like to work for one church, my heart seems to be for many. The Lord also told me that I would be instrumental in building a bridge for unity (hopefully to see John 17 come to pass).

In Him,
Phoebe

Hi Greg,

Again, I have to ask questions in order to know His Truth, so I asked the Lord this question: "Why are there so many Christian denominations?" And the Lord's response: "Seek Me first." As I was pondering His response I wanted to know His definition of division, so I asked the Lord and His response was this: "Division comes from pride—the spirit of pride always comes before Me." He told me that He needs all the Christian churches. When I asked why the Lord told me that every church has a task and He needs them all to set up His kingdom in unity.

My prayer is for all leaders to seek the Lord first so they will know the heart of Jesus. I was told to pray for specific people months ago, and they are Luis Palau, Condoleezza Rice, and again you, Greg. Why the national security adviser? Only God knows. Well, Condoleezza has been under a lot of scrutiny lately. I had a dream that you were becoming more and more prominent and I was becoming less and less. I also had a disturbing vision of firemen scurrying about to put out this massive fire. I keep hearing Proverbs 22:6 (NKJV): "Train up a child in the way he should go, and when he is old he will not depart from it." Salvation comes from within (Jesus), so wake up from the matrix, which is the world. 1 Peter 1:3 this morning and John 3:3.

In Christ,
Phoebe

Hi Greg,

I have been up for over an hour contemplating if I should write. Monday morning I awoke at 2:05. The Lord was inspiring me to write as many things were on my heart, but I wanted to disconnect from you spiritually. Whatever is happening is happening for God's glory. I don't understand the significance of these dreams, visions, and messages, but I do know that I love the Lord with all my heart and that is enough for now. I have to keep moving forward regardless of how I feel, and I have to be more open to what the Lord wants me to do.

Ephesians 4

In Christ,
Phoebe

Hi Greg,

I had three visions that I would like to share with you. About two months ago I had a vision in which I was on a ship. It was dark and rainy and I was drenched, standing on the deck. I saw many people running and confused. Many people came to me and I was helping them get into a smaller boat much like the *Titanic* scene. People were scared and I kept telling them not to worry and that everything would be fine but they had to get into the small boat. When I awoke from this dream I heard this statement from the Lord: "You are ushering people in."

Later I had another vision. In this vision I was standing still looking ahead and I saw flames of fire coming straight at me. Suddenly I felt this presence behind me, and I turned around and saw Jesus. I ran to Him and hid behind Him so the flames wouldn't hit me. But as I was running towards Him I transformed into a child. When I got behind Jesus I held onto His garment in fright. I started feeling safe and I wondered what happened to the flames, so I peeked around Jesus' waist and the flames were still coming but never touching Jesus. Jesus then turned around, looked me in the eyes, and said: "Wake up, O sleepyhead; you have the Spirit of God within you." I then transformed into an adult and walked beside Jesus holding hands.

As we were walking I saw a brilliant light ahead of us, and this light was so brilliant that I hardly noticed these little flames all around us; I remained focused on the light ahead of us. These flames represented the spirits of rejection, cynicism, hatred, intimidation, condemnation, unbelief, lies, insecurities, etc.

My last vision took place over a week ago. I was on a big ship (again like the *Titanic*) and it was a beautiful sunny day. I felt the warmth of the sun penetrating my soul, and I wanted this moment to last. I then walked to the edge of the boat and looked down. What I saw frightened me: thousands and thousands of people in the water drowning. All these people were trying to stay afloat, and their heads kept bobbing up and down. In my spirit I heard: "If you had a choice to help them would you?"

What is so apparent to me is that when I am in the most uncomfortable situation I'm not comfortable talking to people about the Lord. In life we all seem to be somewhere "in or out" of the boat, but no matter where we are we need to keep saving lives with Christ. We have a victorious war going on and God is making sure of that. Remember that God is always for those who choose Him.

About three years ago the previous pastor and I had a confrontation, and afterwards I went home crushed and devastated. I remember lying on the couch in a fetal position crying on and off for twenty-four hours. The pain of rejection was excruciating, but I have never felt closer to the Lord. He gave me beautiful dreams and visions, and He spoke through my husband and children. I felt His presence so powerfully. He renewed my spirit, faith, strength, hope, and love, and I will never forget that. I guess I could have become bitter through my suffering, but the Lord helped me become better.

Towards the end of that twenty-four-hour ordeal I remember asking God, "Why would You connect me with someone like that? Why can't You connect me with someone who is humble, loving, and strong in his (or her) convictions, someone who will sit on a chair and humbly speak to the congregation from his heart? Someone who truly knows and loves You - please connect me with someone like that."

Thank you for sitting in that chair, Greg. I would like to add one more thing: The Lord told me that I can go by feelings if they are righteous in Him. Remember what the Lord told me: "Rise up, O sleepyhead; you have the Spirit [power] of God within you." Scriptures God wants me to keep in my heart: Acts 18, John 3:17, and 1 Peter 2.

God gave us imagination and God wants us to use our imagination for His purposes. "Imagination is more important than knowledge. For knowledge is limited to all we now know and understand, while imagination embraces the entire world, and all there ever will be to know and understand." ~Albert Einstein

Your sister in Christ,
Phoebe

Hi Greg,

It is through Christ's love we find our love, hope, existence, and freedom. Can you imagine those who do not experience this kind of love or even reject it? (This is a glimpse of hell.) I pray for so many lost and hopeless people. I want to give hope to the hopeless through Jesus Christ our Lord. I don't know how God intends to "use" me but the other day when I was praying I told God that I am willing to be used by Him in whatever circumstance; 1 Kings 3:2-15 came to me. I know that it takes a conscious effort to walk in His way, and every day I do struggle with this. The Lord is always patiently waiting and helping me through any struggles. The Lord loves me and is always with me, never to leave me nor forsake me, and I will be with Him throughout eternity. That is the truth!

About a year ago God revealed a vision to me about you (Greg). He wanted me to understand you so He showed me a vision, and what I saw was a little boy's arms going up and down as he was jumping and saying, "Look at me; look what I can do!" But people hardly noticed and didn't seem to care. I felt pain with this vision, a pain of loneliness accompanied with "not feeling loved." What I was told was that you wanted attention so you would do things to get it. I was told that you felt you were never good enough so you would try to get attention in different ways. There was a longing for your dad to be proud of you so you achieved this attention academically. (That is all that was revealed.)

I don't know why God reveals things to me, but what I do know is that God doesn't want me to judge people; He wants me to show compassion for them. In regards to the ordeal with the previous pastor, God revealed that this person didn't have a very good relationship with females. I was also told that this pastor is following his dad's footsteps: like father like son, as they say. I don't judge anyone; I just try to love people where they are. After all that is what I want.

You know that we are at war and it is not against flesh and blood; it is against the lies of the matrix. The matrix is all about living within the word of lies (truth vs. lies). If I do anything in life I hope it is to help my sisters and brothers know the truth and know who they are in Christ; I want them to escape the matrix and experience the fullness of God. "Know the truth and the truth will set you free!"

Isaiah 30:18

Unity in Christ,
Phoebe

Hi Greg,

Last night I had this vision, and in it I saw how small and insignificant I was to the tremendous power of God. In another vision I saw a tree sprouting up at a fast pace. Last week I was thinking about how we as Christians are somewhere on a ship doing our job for His kingdom, and I heard: "You are the rudder" (only if Jesus is driving the boat.) I believe we are here to help one another. The gifts given to me from God are not to be hoarded – they are to be shared.

Last Mother's Day my nine-year-old son came home with a gift. This gift was a picture of him with a message that said "I love my mom because she helps people." I do love to help people—especially to help them break free from bondage. Evil is just a force but we are with a greater force. We as Christians need to know and believe that by the power of the Holy Spirit we can push back the forces of evil, the powers of darkness. And it is by the power of the Holy Spirit that we can accomplish good over evil and light over darkness. I have the faith to believe that by the power of God, we as His children will unite as a force of good to further His kingdom on earth as it is in heaven. The gift of God is eternal life through Jesus Christ our Lord.

Psalm 51, Romans 4 & 6, Matthew 7, Luke 24

In His truth,
Phoebe

Hi Greg,

I was told by the Lord to share in people's burdens. Even though I may not know all of the circumstances, I am supposed to be light and salt to anyone I meet. Many people are blinded and I need to reflect God's love towards them. Even if people hate me, I still need to be light and salt and live in love and truth. Jesus took upon Himself the sins of the world – everybody's sins. Scriptures to meditate on in my heart: John 13 and Matthew 9.

In His grace,
Phoebe

Hi Greg,

I had an unusual dream that had to do with my belief. In this dream I sat up in my bed and Satan was speaking to me through the television. He was speaking with words that no child should hear, and at the very end of his clever speech he told me that he was going to kill my family. I called him a liar and told him that I was going to pray against everything he does. He then fled and I woke up. When I woke up I felt this power within—a power that I never felt before. I was no longer afraid of Satan's tactics. Satan has no power over us when we have the truth in us; he will flee. This is the power we have in Christ, to stand firm in the truth and to pray against the darkness with Jesus' authority, His Word. (Electromagnetic waves to the subconscious mind result in programming the brain to the world's existence. It's like the air we breathe; we don't see it but the effects are astronomical or astrophysical.)

I also had another unusual dream. I was looking at all the blades of grass on the ground when suddenly I saw people rising in the Spirit from each blade of grass. (God wants to raise up a spiritual army.)

I had another beautiful vision, and in this vision I saw Jesus dying on the cross. In the moment of His death I saw a beautiful light coming from His heart, and this light shone upon the whole earth. Jesus told me that the power we speak of is love. The power we speak of is not a power of coercion; it is the power of love that is life-giving and life-changing. God is love, and love holds no record of right and wrong. Love has no gender or color, and the Spirit of love is within all of us. We just have to pursue this love from God.

I remember some of the questions I asked Jesus in the beginning of my journey. I asked Him how He endured such a tortuous death. He told me that He did it for love. Another question I had was why He chose me for this task—there are so many other people who are more qualified than I. I couldn't figure out why He would choose me, so I had to ask Him: "Why me – I don't even know the Bible?" I will never forget the words He spoke to me: "You love Me like you love no other." It's all about loving Jesus first. He can do all things through each believer who loves Him. Scriptures: Luke 6, Mark 9, Zephaniah 3

Here are some messages I received from the Holy Spirit:

- "Invest in the kingdom for there will be eternal consequences."

- "Maximize God; minimize Satan."

- "Forgive, for you will be forgiven."

- "The spirit of legalism is killing the Spirit of My church."

- "Balance is different for everyone"

- "Enjoy life by enjoying Me."

- "Those who see you are in pride; those who see Me are in humility. Do not worry about those who say all kinds of things about you."

- "Do not worry about what the world offers because it doesn't offer Me."

- "Understanding the authority of My power brings humility."

I received a message about three years ago that had to do with the church; this message keeps coming up: "The church of Jesus Christ is under attack, and some will rise and some will fall. For the ones who will rise will rise and the ones who will fall will fall – pray for one another. Some will come in My name but I will not know them. Know My heart so you will not be deceived."

Everyone has the freedom to choose – choose wisely.

Here are some strategies that can help – these instructions are imperative:

1.   Seek the Lord first

2.   Repent

3.   Come together under His authority

4.   Pray

Paul Harvey wrote this essay in 1964.

'If I Were the Devil'…

I wouldn't be happy until I had seized the ripest apple on the tree. Thee,

So I would set about however necessary to take over the United States. I'd subvert the Churches first. I'd begin with a campaign of whispers; with the wisdom of a serpent I would whisper to you as I whispered to Eve: "do as you please". To the young I would whisper that the Bible is a Myth; I would convince them that man created God instead of the other way around. I would confide that what's bad is good and what's good is square. And to the old I would teach to pray after me: our father which art in Washington.

And then I'd get organized, I'd educate authors in how to make lurid literature exciting so that anything else would appear dull and uninteresting, I'd threaten TV with dirtier movies and vice-a-versa, I'd peddle narcotics to whom I could, I'd sell alcohol to ladies and gentlemen of distinction, I'd tranquilize the rest with pills.

If I were the devil I'd soon have families at war with themselves, churches at war with themselves and nations at war with themselves until each in its turn was consumed. And with promises of higher ratings I'd have mesmerizing media fanning the flames.

If I were the devil I would encourage schools to refine young intellect's; but neglect to discipline emotions, just let those run wild until before you knew it, you'd have to have drug sniffing dogs and metal detectors at every schoolhouse door. Within a decade I'd have prisons over flowing, I'd have judges promoting pornography. Soon I could evict GOD from the courthouse, then from the schoolhouse and then from the houses of congress. And in his own churches I would substitute psychology for religion and deify science. I would lure priests and pastors into misusing boys and girls and church money.

If I were the devil I'd make the symbol of Easter an egg, and the symbol of Christmas a bottle. If I were the devil I'd take from those who have and give to those who wanted until I had killed the incentive of the ambitious. And what will you bet I couldn't get whole states to promote gambling as the way to get rich. I would caution against extremes in hard work, in patriotism, in moral conduct. I would convince the young that marriage is old-fashioned, that swinging is more fun, that what you see on TV is the way to be; and thus I could undress you in public, and I could lure you into bed with diseases for which there is no cure. In other words if I were the devil, I'd just keep on doing what he's doing.

Do you know what excites me? It is not a new car or a new house or anything that this world has to offer; it is the love and truth that I receive from the Lord. Also, I get excited when I see the scales coming off people's eyes and they start experiencing the love and truth of the Lord.

Scriptures: Matthew 3:3 and Philippians 3:8

In Christ,
Phoebe

Hi Greg,

I had two visions a couple of weeks ago. The first vision was about Jesus as the Good Shepherd. He had a staff in His right hand, and He was looking down at all of His sheep. His sheep were scrambling all over, as if they could not recognize Jesus as the Good Shepherd. In the other vision I saw Jesus peacefully sitting on a rock overlooking Jerusalem. The Lord told me that when He does come back it is going to be with great vengeance and judgment. He wants us to be prepared for this—whenever it will take place. He wants His people to know His love and truth because without this we surely will perish.

More messages from the Lord:

- "Attain the glory of the Lord."

- "Seek love first for this will bring unity which will glorify Me."

- "Glory to glory"

- "I can perform all kinds of miracles, but I would rather see love."

- "Perfect love casts out all fear."

I started a prayer chain in my neighborhood. There are opportunities all around us, but we must be open to them. Reaching out to people is just releasing His love. Fear is just a fine veneer, a thin layer that God's love can break through.

Mark 7, Proverbs 3:3, Ezekiel 38, Jeremiah 1, Galatians 6

Peace and love,
Phoebe

Hi Greg,

On November 1 I was awakened at 3:03 a.m. and heard the name Eve. In response I said, "Eve? I am not Eve." And then I heard: "Pray!" The next morning I was awakened again at 3:00 and told to pray. Now I am periodically waking up around 3:00 and I hear the word "pray." These are the words spoken to me in regards to certain circumstances:

- "Prayer and patience"

- "Be more committed"

- "Remain faithful"

- "Work together"

- "The position you are in is better to make peace and not war"

- "I am in the business of restoration"

- "Strive for the goal that I have set before you"

- "To whom much is given much will be expected"

- "If you were alone, cold, and naked would I be enough?"

- "I am the one who supplies all of your needs"

In a dream I saw a little lady in a light blue habit working very hard. (She was working so hard and yet she never tired.) When she turned around she looked at me with a great big smile, and it was Mother Teresa. She was so beautiful; she had this intense light that radiated from her.

Wednesday night I had a vision right before I fell asleep. I saw a multitude of angels, and they all seemed to have a purpose. I know that we are not alone. I woke up Thursday morning at 3:00 and heard John 1:14 in my spirit. I was told to take this to heart and then to pray. I would like to share with you the first divine dream I had: I was sleeping in bed when this androgynous angel woke me up. He/she took me up to heaven and said, "This is for you." The scenery was so beautiful. Heaven looked like earth but much more beautiful; it was so shiny it glistened. The colors were more beautiful than any colors on earth. The colors blue and green were indescribable. I felt like I was in a New World. While I stood gazing at the beautiful scene I noticed a stream ahead of me. I ran to it and looked over the embankment and saw this beautiful water that reflected the colors of the rainbow. I then awoke from my dream.

Psalm 33, Matthew 24, Psalm 56

In Him,
Phoebe

Hi Greg,

I finally received the meaning of Eve: "The bride of Christ; it is for all those who come into repentance." Then I received 1 Timothy 2. Four years ago God told me to come under your presence. God does use women to teach as it is He who is doing the teaching. God believes in you as your heart is pliable.

More messages from our Lord:

- "Love covers a multitude of sins."

- "Your reward is in heaven."

- "Pray without ceasing."

- "Do you know what makes you different from the animals? You can pray."

- "Focus on your destiny."

I had some interesting visions: I saw the apostles walking on a high and narrow bridge. I saw Jesus praying and looking down at the water from the bridge with a dove fluttering about. I had another vision that disturbed me about three weeks ago. In it I saw a lot of people in military uniform getting ready for battle.

My son also had a disturbing dream that woke him up. Cole tapped me on the shoulder crying. All he said was "Blake died." He went on to tell me that he didn't know how his brother died but that he died in his dream. Well, I am praying against this one in Jesus' name. Out of all five of my kids Blake teaches me the most – he reminds me of Jesus in how he conducts his life. When he was five he sat next to me on the couch early one morning and told me that Jesus is coming back. He proceeded to tell me that Jesus is going to take the people down there (as he pointed to the floor) first and then He is going to take the rest of us. He told me that the devil is going to make everyone believe he is nice – then he is going to cut their heads, arms, and legs off.

Blake went on to tell me that Jesus had to fight the devil and He won. He told me that the earth is going to open up and the houses and cars will fall into the earth. He said there will be fire everywhere. I asked him how he knew this, and matter-of-factly he said that God told him in the middle of the night. Around that time Blake saw an angel outside our house. He would point to him and say, "Don't you see him? He's right there."

Why am I telling you this? I don't know. This was four years ago. I told this to the previous pastor, but his only response was "Come on, a five-year-old child?" I almost said, "Well, if He can speak through a jackass, He certainly can speak through a five-year-old child." I just walked away. This was a pivotal time when I decided not to enter this church again and let go and let God do His work.

Do you know what the best gift we can give to one another? It is that we love and believing in one another. God loves and believes in us—we should love and believe in one another. God bless and Merry Christmas.

Ephesians 3:17

In Him,
Phoebe

Here is one way we could learn how to teach one another (written by Elizabeth Silance Ballard):

"Three Letters from Teddy"

As she stood in front of her 5th grade class on the very first day of school, she told the children an untruth. Like most teachers, she looked at her students and said that she loved them all the same. However, that was impossible, because there in the front row, slumped in his seat, was a little boy named Teddy Stoddard.

Mrs. Thompson had watched Teddy the year before and noticed that he did not play well with the other children, that his clothes were messy and that he constantly needed a bath. In addition, Teddy could be unpleasant. It got to the point where Mrs. Thompson would actually take delight in marking his papers with a broad red pen, making bold X's and then putting a big "F" at the top of his papers.

At the school where Mrs. Thompson taught, she was required to review each child's past records and she put Teddy's off until last. However, when she reviewed his file, she was in for a surprise.

Teddy's first grade teacher wrote, "Teddy is a bright child with a ready laugh. He does his work neatly and has good manners... he is a joy to be around...." His second grade teacher wrote, "Teddy is an excellent student, well-liked by his classmates, but he is troubled because his mother has a terminal illness and life at home must be a struggle." His third grade teacher wrote, "His mother's death has been hard on him. He tries to do his best, but his father doesn't show much interest and his home life will soon affect him if some steps aren't taken." Teddy's fourth grade teacher wrote, "Teddy is withdrawn and doesn't show much interest in school. He doesn't have many friends and he sometimes sleeps in class."

By now, Mrs. Thompson realized the problem and she was ashamed of herself. She felt even worse when her students brought her Christmas presents, wrapped in beautiful ribbons and bright paper, except for Teddy's. His present was clumsily wrapped in the heavy brown paper that he got from a grocery bag. Mrs. Thompson took pains to open it in the middle of the other presents.

Some of the children started to laugh when she found a rhinestone bracelet with some of the stones missing and a bottle that was one-quarter full of perfume. But she stifled the children's laughter when she exclaimed how pretty the bracelet was, putting it on, and dabbing some of the perfume on her wrist.

Teddy Stoddard stayed after school that day just long enough to say, "Mrs. Thompson, today you smelled just like my Mom used to." After the children left, she cried for at least an hour.

On that very day, she quit teaching reading, writing and arithmetic. Instead, she began to teach children. Mrs. Thompson paid particular attention to Teddy. As she worked with him, his mind seemed to come alive. The more she encouraged him, the faster he responded. By the end of the year, Teddy had become one of the smartest children in the class and, despite her lie that she would love all the children the same, Teddy became one of her "teacher's pets."

A year later, she found a note under her door, from Teddy, telling her that she was still the best teacher he ever had in his whole life. Six years went by before she got another note from Teddy. He then wrote that he had finished high school, third in his class, and she was still the best teacher he ever had in life.

Four years after that, she got another letter, saying that while things had been tough at times, he'd stayed in school, had stuck with it, and would soon graduate from college with the highest of honors. He assured Mrs. Thompson that she was still the best and favorite teacher he had ever had in his whole life.

Then four more years passed and yet another letter came. This time he explained that after he got his bachelor's degree, he decided to go a little further. The letter explained that she was still the best and favorite teacher he ever had. But now his name was a little longer. The letter was signed, Theodore F. Stoddard, MD.

The story does not end there. You see, there was yet another letter that spring. Teddy said he had met this girl and was going to be married. He explained that his father had died a couple of years ago and he was wondering if Mrs. Thompson might agree to sit at the wedding in the place that was usually reserved for the mother of the groom. Of course, Mrs. Thompson did. And guess what? She wore that bracelet, the one with several rhinestones missing. Moreover, she made sure she was wearing the perfume that Teddy remembered his mother wearing on their last Christmas together.

They hugged each other, and Dr. Stoddard whispered in Mrs. Thompson's ear, "Thank you Mrs. Thompson for believing in me. Thank you so much for making me feel important and showing me that I could make a difference."

Mrs. Thompson, with tears in her eyes, whispered back. She said, "Teddy, you have it all wrong. You were the one who taught me that I could make a difference. I didn't know how to teach until I met you!"

(For those of you who don't know, Teddy Stoddard is the doctor at Iowa Methodist in Des Moines that has the Stoddard Cancer Wing.)

Hi Greg,

Last week I had a vision of a burning bush. On Saturday (Christmas) I kept hearing the word *macabre* all day. That evening I had a vision of clouds in the sky, and then on Sunday I had another vision of an angel blowing a beautiful golden trumpet. I didn't feel that this vision was urgent.

About a month ago I had a vision that I only shared with my friends; I didn't understand it so I didn't dwell on it. In this vision I kept seeing people coming up from the water, and they were all dead. The ocean kept bringing in dead bodies, and there were so many bodies washed up on shore that people were lining them up—rows and rows of dead people lined up on the shoreline. I really didn't understand this so I confided to my Bible study friends that maybe a ship will capsize and many people will drown and wash up on shore; then the tsunami hit.

So many more incidents have occurred that I have only confessed to my husband and close friends. One in particular I now feel I have to share. On September 10, 2001, I remember having a hard time sleeping. I went to bed at 10 p.m., and every time I closed my eyes I kept seeing visuals of burnt people. This vision was one like I never had before—like a movie projector moving at a very fast pace. I kept seeing burnt people and then a black police officer, a mother and daughter, and more burnt people. When I opened my eyes I felt this peaceful presence in my room, and I said "I don't understand." Every time I closed my eyes the visions became more disturbing so I took melatonin in order to get some sleep.

The next morning I watched in horror at what happened to New York. I was also told that California would have several earthquakes, and one would be devastating—when I do not know.

Amos 7, 2 Peter 3, Matthew 23, 1 Corinthians 3:3, 13

More messages from the Lord:

- "Most of the leaders of My church are full of pride – teach them humility as this will separate the wheat from the chaff."

- "Humility brings unity."

- "Have faith rather than fear."

- "Live by faith not by sight."

- "Remain in peace and live in love."

- "What can I do for you?" This is what I heard: "love."

I am sending you another letter that I wrote earlier but hesitated to send.

When God told me that He was going to make me an example to the church, and not knowing how He was going to do this, I signed up. (I counted the cost before I signed – not my family.) But in order for me to say yes I asked God to honor me with the love and support I need from my husband, and as a team we would venture through whatever God has chosen for us. God has honored my request.

So why am I at Woodland Hills Church? God told me to attend WHC and come under you, Greg. That is why I am at your church. After worship on Sunday I was thinking about disconnecting from the church altogether as I felt that I wasn't making any difference and was wasting my time. I asked my husband his advice and he told me to continue obeying the Lord as I am only to deliver messages; he told me that I needed to allow God to change the hearts of His people. I said, "If God is using me in this way why am I so miserable?" He responded, "That is your own choice. God has blessed you; He has blessed us." He also told me that my biggest problem is that I always want to see immediate results after I deliver a message. My husband reminded me that I may not see any results for two or three years, and I have to keep God's timing in perspective.

As I was thinking about letting go of church altogether a close friend called me. She told me that she had an explicit dream about me, and the dream was about not giving up. Later on that day my seven-year-old daughter was watching cartoons when out of the blue she started singing "Amazing Grace." God has me covered everywhere I turn. Later that evening I was told that my heart was growing hard because I was not listening with spiritual ears. Sometimes I wonder why I continue because I know what I am up against – it's called conformity, conformity of the world and not of the Spirit. But knowing that this is not my home and that God is on my side, I can continue.

I had another vision of a burning bush, and later that day I tuned into a Christian talk show where the pastor talked about how Moses did not do what God asked him to do. God told him to command water from the rock, yet Moses struck the rock with his staff instead. Because of Moses' disobedience and lack of trust, he never saw the Promised Land.

Matthew 25, Amos 7

In Christ,
Phoebe

Hi Greg,

God is all-powerful and all-loving. God is not bound by time – He is always present in Jesus Christ. You asked me a question that I had to ponder: these visions I receive are not only to experience the Truth; they are meant to prepare me for what is to come – and pray. All I know is that prayer is powerful and I have seen miracles happen through prayer.

One morning while I was watching the international news story about the tsunami and crying for all those suffering God gave me a peaceful vision. In this vision I saw thousands of spirits going straight up. I was then told to help and pray for those left behind. Scripture to ponder: 1 Corinthians 13, 1 Thessalonians 2, 1 Thessalonians 3:12, and Acts 2.

In His love,
Phoebe

Hi Greg,

Here's a rhetorical question. If you did an empirical study and asked the question "How many times do you see God working in your life versus not at all?" how do you think people would respond? The truth of the matter is that God is always working in our lives, and the question is do we know Him well enough to notice and be aware of His existence?

I just want to express one more thing that persistently bothers me about some churches. When I venture to different churches some of the pastors make God too holy for any of us. On a hierarchical level it would always be God on top, and then the pastors, and then the deacons, and so on. But in truth His leadership is reversed. The first is last and the last is first. God came down to our level to show His love for us and to serve with humility. Why do you think He did this? He wants to connect with us on a personal level. He is our one true and only leader.

God is holy, but more importantly He has a personal love for each one of us, and He already proved this. God is our Creator who loves us all, and I pray that more people will know this love. Scriptures to sink into my heart: Jude 1:17-25, John 4:10, 1 Corinthians 16: 9, 1 Corinthians 12:11, and 1 John 3:20.

In His living Word,
Phoebe

Hi Greg,

The other day I was thinking how wonderful it is that God's Holy Spirit is making me a better parent, spouse, and friend. He creates a healthy balance to my life, and I lean upon Him for help and understanding. I can see that my children are becoming healthy well-balanced individuals. These children do not belong to me, and I want to do whatever I can to make the truth known to them. I don't expect perfection from them because that is not my job. My part is to teach them the truth and pray that the Holy Spirit will develop them into what He created them to be.

I counsel a lot of people, and too many times we want outside perfection from ourselves and from others. Do you know what you get when you expect perfection? You get disappointment. You also get behaviors like oppositional defiant disorder or worse yet obsessive-compulsive disorder, and these are only a few personality disorders that manifest. This world focuses on the outside behavior. If you want someone to change it has to start from the inside out. God judges the heart while we tend to judge on the outside behavior. As a parent I want my children to have a foundation built on the truth of God, and if they make a mistake I will be there to get them back on the right track.

I can't fault anyone for the choices they make because I am guilty of the same mistake. We're all not perfect – we all sin, but it is by His grace that we can be forgiven and start anew. As children of God it is our job to help and encourage others and see them as Christ-ones. We need to let people make their own choices in life and hope and pray they will come to know Christ and develop into Him. Everyone has a potential to become a Christ-one, and it is our job is to make this known. This is a battle yet to be won.

What's ironic is that we have become so oblivious to the lies that surround us and we accept these lies as truth—we have settled for the mediocre. This is why God so desperately wants us to wake us up to this truth. Being born again is just waking up to the truth of who Christ is and understanding who we are in Christ. This is a new birth, a new beginning – this is the first step to acknowledging the Truth. It is the power of His Holy Spirit that helps us do this. It is by His grace that we are saved and it is by His grace that we can become like the Holy One.

This is the way I look at people. We are all gifts individually wrapped ready to give ourselves to one another. No matter what the content – Jesus is inside. When we realize that people are a gift from God and God loves everyone, we really can sincerely love and help people. God is the composer – we are the ones playing a beautiful instrument. When God composes music we all get to play a part and help create a beautiful symphony.

I want to share more experiences with you as we progress in this journey with our Lord. About a month ago, one of the sisters in our group mentioned a vision she had about me five years ago. She told me God wanted her to know I was going through spiritual warfare and needed prayer. In this vision she saw a grotesque creature that looked somewhat like a lion pacing back and forth, and then it turned and hissed at her. At the time, she didn't really know me or know what I was going through so she never mentioned it until now. I do remember going through many battles at that time. I can honestly say I never want to go through all I had to endure at that time, but I am actually glad that I did because without all those battles I could not battle what I am battling today.

People need to know that we are all in a spiritual battle, and it is not over until Jesus' return. I am only bringing these experiences to light because I want people informed of what is truly going on. We need to be aware that there is a ruler to this world, and we need to put on the armor of God and the breastplate of righteousness. Know who you are in Christ.

I keep having this reoccurring vision: I see large groups of people, many of whom look confused or as if they are waiting for something. I had another vision a week ago: I was in this beautiful place and Jesus was waiting for me. I walked towards Him and bowed down before Him, and He laid a crown upon my head and said: "This is your crown of life." I wonder what I have to endure before I get there. All I know is that I know where I am going to end up, so whatever happens to me until then I will be content.

Colossians 3:17

In Christ,
Phoebe

Hi Greg,

Right after I sent you a recent letter I received a message from the Lord, and this is what I heard: "Phoebe, you are putting on your old way of thinking (old wine skin). Remember, people are blind and they need to know the truth in love. Let love overshadow all other emotions. Let love be your highest source." I love the Lord so much because He talks to me with such love, compassion, kindness, and understanding. He never talks to me with cynicism, corruption, condemnation, or accusation. HE IS ALL-LOVING, and I am glad that I can put my trust "souly" in Him. God is guarding and guiding my heart. The people who know me the best know that I have a loving and forgiving heart. I am not perfect, but if I ever get upset (hurt) about anything just know that it only lasts for a moment. I just need time to think things through and hear from God. If I am to be an example to the church, I have to be as transparent as I can be—after all I am a realist. After I read your response the next day all I could think of is that I need to dwell on unity not division.

Now I will share an unusual vision that I received last week. In this vision I saw Satan standing two feet from me, and he was looking directly into my eyes for about five minutes, as if he were studying me. His eyes were a clear solid blue, and he took on a human form. I knew who he was and for some reason he knew who I was. After staring at me for five minutes he took a step forward and his eyes shifted to solid black and he took on a more grotesque form. Then he started to walk around me sensing everything about me. While he proceeded to walk around me the Lord appeared and told Satan that he could not have me, and He told him to go back to the lake of fire. Then Satan became fire and he was gone. (I know the lake of fire is prepared for him in the end but this is what I saw and heard.)

The Lord spoke to me and said, "Satan is trying to instill fear within you so that you will become paralyzed and not proceed forward." The Lord told me this is one of Satan's strategies among God's chosen people. He told me not to fear for He is always with me, and then the vision was gone. Our warfare is not against flesh and blood, it is against the spirits in the spiritual realms. But the Lord can rebuke Satan and he has to listen!

Deep down I really don't want to be persecuted, nor do I want to be hurt, but I know this is part of being a disciple of Christ because standing for truth and love is not always easy. I do know that when I am advancing His kingdom it gets riskier, and therefore I seem to try to find a reason to quit. A couple of weeks ago I asked God if He would just let me be and let me raise my kids. But of course He is leading me in another direction. I know I have to trust God, and I realize that He is with me ALWAYS. Every time I think God is done with me He tells me that He is just starting. And every time I ask God what I should do next He tells me to just be.

In Him,
Phoebe

Hi Greg,

Over four years ago I went to God for answers. I wanted to know the truth about who He is. I was getting so many different opinions from different pastors that I became very confused about who God is and what is right and what is wrong. Is there predestination? What does baptism really mean? Sacraments or not? Pre, mid, or post? Who gets saved and who doesn't? So many questions – the Baptists believe this and the Catholics believe that, and so on and so on. One night I remember going to God out of desperation. Knowing that I have sinned against Him, I felt that I needed to reach out to Him just to clear the air and confess everything. Because of what was being preached from the pulpit I thought I was doomed for hell.

I remember going in my closet and getting real with God. That night I exposed everything that was hidden—I had so much shame and guilt I wanted God to see me in that. I have hurt people in the past and mostly I have hurt myself and God – I wanted everything exposed. At that time I was willing to give it all to God, and I asked Him to use me in any way He wanted. I did this periodically, and for some reason the more I did this the less shame and guilt I felt. God heard me and started to communicate with me in various ways.

In one incident I told God I was sorry because I felt that I was not giving enough money to the church and I occasionally drink wine with my friends—I thought I was going to hell for this. As I was falling into a deep sleep God gave me this beautiful picture: I was in a white bridal dress that had no stain, wrinkle, or blemish—I was so radiant and beautiful. I woke up and said, "I am going to heaven!"

I was so excited that God loved me and saw me as a radiant bride. At that point I drew a line in the sand and no longer listened to preachers preaching about **their** judgments and condemnation. I felt free to be myself, and I could come to God with whatever I wanted. That trust was open for me and I started to trust Him with everything. God was giving me His truth whereas man was giving me many different truths. I decided from then on that I would only trust God with His Truth; I would trust Him with everything.

I have learned over the years that I can come to my Father with anything and know that He cares and is listening to me. I matter to Him and He wants to show me how much He loves me. I cherish our relationship more than anything on earth because He gave me hope where I thought there was no hope at all. Now I have a heart to speak to people about God's love, grace, truth, forgiveness, repentance, and unity, especially to those who don't know Him. I have a heart to reach people about what God has done on the cross for us – His saving grace. He took our sins so that we may have a loving and trusting relationship with Him, and He wants us to spend all eternity with Him. When you see Jesus you see the love of God. There is too much judgment, condemnation, cynicism, and opinion being preached from the pulpit, and it makes people turn away from God. This is why my brother went from loving Jesus to becoming a Buddhist.

I pray that preachers will seek God first and just preach about His love, truth, and unity. We all know about His wrath so we should let Him deal with hell. We have to trust God in all of this and know that He is in control. We are all at different levels, and we need to let the Holy Spirit breathe and move in our lives. Let all the petty differences go and love God and share His love with others so that we can build His kingdom in unity: John 17. Let Jesus be the rightful judge. We all have particulars but we should not let these particulars come between loving God, ourselves, and our neighbors – let go and let God.

As we are all in the process of transformation, it is only right to give each other grace. We are all dead without Christ. Everything that God has been doing through me is small in comparison to what Jesus did on the cross. The foundation has been laid; we just have to build on it – this is a process.

I also want to add a couple of visions I received four years ago (in 2000). I saw Mary twice and couldn't figure out why I was receiving visions about her. In the first vision Mary was looking at the world, and I felt a lot of emotions coming from her. She seemed very sad for the world; she had so much sadness that I started to weep. In another vision I saw Mary praying to God—she looked about thirteen or fourteen years old, with long dark brown hair. As she was praying I saw such purity and love that it radiated from her to God. She seemed so young and innocent.

Another vision: I saw a tree bearing several different fruits. God told me that He is raising up prophets all over the world. He also told me that I am another Paul. My response was, "Oh, great." He said that I would suffer but it would be different. He keeps telling me to clothe myself with humility because I will not bear fruit without doing this.

More messages from the Lord:

- "I require obedience more than sacrifice."

- "Keep your focus on the things that matter to Me."

- "Doubt perpetuates fear – keep the faith in your mind, heart, and soul."

- "This is the day that the Lord has made so rejoice and be glad in it."

Do you know what I would like to see coming from the pulpit? I would love to hear from the homeless, prostitutes, criminals, and addicts. I would love to hear how God has transformed them and what God is doing through them. The heart is what matters to God. Let's honor Him in this area. Almost every day I work with people who continually suffer, sometimes until death, and I learn so much from them. I would rather be with these people who suffer than with people who are in high places of honor. It's an honor and blessing to share my life with them.

Joel 3, 1 John 3, 1 John 5, Colossians 2, Mark 11:27, 1 Peter 3

For His glory,
Phoebe

Hi Greg,

The Lord has been pressing in on me about more issues in my life. Monday morning as I awoke I was thinking about how wonderful life is to be so blessed with family and friends. The Lord knows that He is always first in my life—well, that is what I thought. That morning He awoke me with some questions. He said, "Would you be willing to sacrifice your life for Me?" My response was, "Lord, you know I would." He then said, "Would you be willing to sacrifice your family for Me?" My response was, "Lord, you know I wouldn't. I would sacrifice *with* my family but not apart from them." Again He said, "Would you be willing to give up everything for Me?" (I seemed to be pulled in both directions.)

I thought about how God tested Abraham with his son, Isaac. I contemplated this dilemma. I remember four years ago sharing a dream I had with Pastor Bill. In this dream my family perished and I was alone. When I found out that my family all died I cried and cried, and I told the Lord that I couldn't go on. An angel appeared and said, "Yes, you can." I said, "No, I can't." And she said, "Yes, you can—you will see them again on the other side." As I was crying and listening to the angel I said, "Yes, I can and I will see them again." And then I awoke.

Ever since then I have had several dreams of me being alone during the end times, and in these dreams (no matter what the circumstances are) I am always telling people that it's not too late to turn their hearts back to the Lord. (It seems to me that in these dreams my family gets taken up and I am always left behind to preach the Good News.) I know the Lord is preparing my heart for something because He keeps giving me these dreams and visions. I know the Lord is with me always—He lives in me and knows my every thought and intention of my heart—but at this point in my life I really don't want to be physically alone. Think about it – would you be willing to give up everything? I am still contemplating and praying.

A couple of weeks ago I received more visions, and in one of these visions I saw a lot of people looking up at the sky waiting for Jesus to return, but what I saw was a wake-up call. These people gazing up at the sky looked alive but their skin was a bluish-gray color. I asked the Lord what this meant and He said: "Many people think they are alive but they are dead."

I was about to doze off the other night when I received another vision. I saw people killing one another, even their own people, and the fighting would not stop. Another vision reflected what we all should become, and it was a big bright beautiful shining star.

1 John 3, Matthew 17, Ephesians 6

In Christ,
Phoebe

I wrote the above earlier and a dramatic change took place in my heart since then. While I was praying and contemplating the question the Lord had laid on my heart I received a vision. In this vision I saw the Lord dying on the cross, and He was so bloody, bruised, and broken. In my mind's eye I saw tears coming down His face. And then I heard: "I gave up everything for you." In an instant the vision was gone. Of course I started crying and my heart began to focus on Jesus and not myself. Well, my heart changed at that moment and I can sincerely say that I am willing to give it all—it's all about love.

A couple of messages that I received:

- "Draw strength from Me."

- "Don't be fooled by titles."

- "God is close to the humble."

- "The spirit of pride is in many of the church leaders."

- "Be at peace with everyone."

Whatever small part God has for me, I will do it with the best of my integrity.

Hebrews 1, Psalm 97

God bless you,
Phoebe

Hi Greg,

A couple of weeks ago you made a statement that I hold in my heart, and that is to always keep your eyes on the Lord. The Lord showed me a vision of Truth. In this vision I saw a clean white slate. I asked the Lord what it meant and He said that whenever I start to judge people to think of this clean white slate with nothing on it. Instead of judging people I am to treat them like it is the first time we met without placing any judgmental thoughts on them. The Lord showed me that this is what He does with me every time I come to Him in repentance – everything is gone except a clean white slate. His mercies are new every morning.

This is what we are to do with everyone. The Lord shows His grace towards us; therefore we should extend that grace towards others. When we do this we are imitating Christ. The joy of the Lord is my strength. Isn't it ironic how some people are willing to give up their lives for their country? What a different world it would be if we had that same attitude and courage for our Lord and Savior. 1 Peter 2:9, Acts 5:41, Philippians 2, Psalm 112

In His service,
Phoebe

Hi Greg,

Last night the Lord had me reflect on two incidents that happened to me about four years ago. I ran a childcare business from the time my first child was born until my last one was in school full-time (thirteen years). In one of the incidents I was outside with the kids when a man came by walking his dog. This man was very out of place. He looked homeless – very thin and very dirty. His hair was all messed up and his clothes were tattered. When I saw him I remember saying to myself that he must be homeless, but I knew I could not judge him by his appearance. As he walked by he was smiling. I said hi and asked him what kind of a dog he had. He answered with this beautiful smile: "It's a cockapoo." I told him that I had two cockapoos and he nodded.

As he was walking by my heart just went out to him and I said, "Have a good day." He replied, "And you too." He had a sparkle in his eyes and displayed such contentment. I went back to sit down then immediately got up to see which direction he was headed, and he was gone – out of sight.

Another incident happened about three or four months later. I was outside with the kids again when I saw this big boisterous man walking in the middle of the road. He was humming and whistling along. He saw me with the kids and said with this big smile: "It's a beautiful day isn't it?" His countenance was one of joy and bliss. This seemed like another strange incident because no one walks in the middle of the road. I had never seen him before (just like the other man). This guy was about 280 pounds and stood about 6-foot-7. He looked to be a man in his 60s.

Anyway, after he asked me that question I answered, "Yes, it is a beautiful day." He kept humming along and singing as if he had no cares in the world. I wondered if he was mentally unstable, and I started to get worried because if he were I would have to protect him.

It's ironic that now I am working with people who are poor and some with mental health issues.

I received another message from the Lord, and He said He wants His church to be like a hospital. Something tells me that if we ran God's church like a hospital then people of all ages, races, and genders would come. You don't see a Latino hospital or a hospital just for African Americans. Doctors and nurses of all races and colors come together to work and to bring their gifts and talents to help the hurt, lost, sick, suffering, and dying. I was also shown a very weird vision: I saw Satan wearing some kind of wedding headgear. I asked the Lord what this meant and He said that Satan is trying to replicate the bride of Christ, His church.

Daniel, Philippians 1, Philippians 2:3, Psalm 46

Resting in God's peace,
Phoebe

Hi Greg,

When God told me to take my family to a certain church I didn't have any idea why. I didn't want to go to this church because of my past unresolved issues related to this religion, issuing from my childhood. You see, I grew up with this religion, but after my mom and dad divorced when I was eight my family was excommunicated. We were told that we could come to church but not participate in communion. My mom told the priest, "What you're saying to me is that you are inviting us to dinner but we can't eat." She went on to say that if she were a lost sheep in this world Jesus would be looking for her.

My mom left this religion and never returned. God told me not to blame the priest because this is what they were taught. There were more issues, but God being so gracious let me understand the bigger picture. God guiding me back to this religion had nothing to do with the religion itself; it had everything to do with connections.

Growing up with my mom was quite the different lifestyle. She took in unwed mothers and later became a foster mom to teenage boys. She used to work at the boy's ranch and the girl's villa (home for delinquent teenagers). I remember her bringing home teenagers to our house for holidays because they didn't have a home to go to. All my life I have been influenced by my mom's love and compassion for others. She exemplified the hands and feet of Jesus. I didn't go to church a lot during my high school years but I saw Christ in action in my home. As I have always said, "I would rather see a sermon than hear one."

Now, looking back, I can understand why I have so much compassion for people who are hurting. I also understand why I always felt unwelcome in church. This is one of the reasons why I went to God in desperation for the Truth. I'm sure there are a lot of people who still get this "unwelcome" impression from Christian churches. I don't think the church today is what Jesus had in mind when He first initiated it. The church should be a church of love, unity, compassion, and humility. Jesus should be the head of the church not man. It would be easier to reach people if the churches set aside their doctrines and connected in the name of Christ.

If we are looking to the world for answers we all will be disappointed. This is why it is imperative one looks at Christ for transformation, not for religious conformation. The church does not make you a Christian, Christ does. The church is there to point to Christ. I love going to church to praise and worship the Lord. I also love communion. This may not be for everyone but it has a lot of meaning to me. You know what is so freeing? Breaking the doctrines of religion and following Christ. With all the religions in the world I have never conformed to one. The principle I have come to understand is that you set your mind free from the world and let your heart be open to God, and all things are possible. All this world offers is self-destruction.

Messages from the Lord:

- "Say no to the seductions of the world."

- "Men are flawed; God is not."

- "Enter My rest."

- "Enjoy your journey with Me."

Matthew 13:33, 1 Corinthians 13, Philippians 3:13, Ephesians 5:16, Psalm 27

Under His grace,
Phoebe

Hi Greg,

I am always careful of leaders in the church who are legalistic. These people put God in a box and only see Him in part. When one wants to see God's fullness one doesn't limit what God can do; don't put Him in a box. God can use the single woman or the married man. God may gift individuals differently, one a doer and the other a supporter. I pray that people will see God in full because when they do, their eyes will be opened. Luke 24:31

In Him,
Phoebe

Hi Greg,

Last Saturday I awoke in the middle of the night from the strangest dream. In this dream I was in a small to midsize airplane, and all of a sudden I was seized by fear and I heard someone say that the pilot was dead. I heard that the co-pilot was dead too and we were flying on auto-pilot. A man asked if anyone on board knew how to fly a plane, and no one came forward. I said: "We are all going to die." And then I woke up from my dream. I thought God was telling me not to go on this trip I have set up for November. I told Craig in the morning about my dream, and then we watched the news and heard what happened to the plane in Greece. I don't know why things like this happen to me—I gather it is to pray.

I've had more visions lately: I saw many people on horseback ready for war. In another vision I saw these strong pillars growing. I also had another vision of many beautiful flowers in a meadow, and they all looked so colorful and beautiful. But when I came up closer to the flowers I saw weeds growing around them, and it was as if the weeds were slowly strangling the flowers.

The Lord also told me that I am a prophet, and the message He wants me to send is this: "I want all of My children to turn their hearts to Me, and I want My children to get along." Didn't you have a vision like this about eighteen months ago? His message is plain and simple – please get this message out. I never considered myself anything but a servant of the Lord, and I want to keep it that way. I hate labels. The Lord is not interested in what gifts He has given – He is interested in what we do with the gifts He has given. Will we remain faithful until the end? The question should never be "Are you saved?" The question should be "Do you have an ongoing personal relationship with the Lord?" Inviting Him in is just the beginning.

Here are more messages:

- "There is power in numbers."

- "The enemy can see that your prayers are effective – pray without ceasing."

- "For every true prophet there will be more counterfeits – be on guard."

- "To recognize the blessing is the blessing, but gratitude for the blessing will last forever."

I woke up Saturday morning with this request from God: "I want to raise up an army that will fight the forces of evil. Come together and I will give you the knowledge and wisdom to do so. Follow your strength and believe it's from Me. Have an appetite for your Lord."

I asked, "Lord, what do You want from us?" His response was Psalm 119.

Psalm 91, Matthew 18, 2 Corinthians 5, Philippians 4

In Him,
Phoebe

Hi Greg,

God is good all the time; all the time God is good. Reading the Old Testament is good only if a person reads it with the lens of Christ; it will give a person a new perspective: All teaching, preaching, and prophecy in the Bible points to Jesus Christ. Whenever people confuse who God is I have to remember that they are stuck in a web of deception (matrix), and I ask the Lord's help in how to lead them to His Truth. We are all at different levels spiritually, and we need one another to help us see the light whenever there is darkness.

I thank God for His Holy Spirit because it is His Spirit that helps us know who we are in Christ, and it is His Spirit that equips us to know how to build His kingdom. I am teaching my kids about this because I don't hear much about it; I really never did.

The other night when I spent time with the Lord He called me the "bride of Christ" – this is for all those who have an intimate relationship with Him. You see, many years ago I boldly went to our Father and asked for His Son's hand in marriage. Accepting Jesus as my Lord and Savior is the best decision I ever made. That night I made a commitment to Him – to love, honor, and cherish Him from this day forward. My Lord takes precedence over anything or anyone in my life. I promised to be loyal and serve Him wherever and whenever He wanted. I told Him that I would give Him my life because I trusted Him. I have a deep intimate relationship with Him, and I am committed to carry out whatever His will is for me. I have to take all others out of the equation because the Lord is what matters to me the most.

Ephesians 6, Ephesians 3:19, Ephesians 4:13

Abiding in His love and peace,
Phoebe

Hi Greg,

Wednesday morning as I was waking up I heard: "I want My body to be connected." The Lord is the Head of the body but His body is disconnected.

I had more visions, and two of them were the same two nights in a row. I kept seeing this dead tree bearing no leaves or fruit. (This started me thinking about the work of the Holy Spirit.) I asked the Lord about all of this – about the infilling and sealing of the Holy Spirit. I wanted to know the truth in regards to this and the Lord said: "You are filled when I say you are filled; you are sealed when I say you are sealed. I am the righteous judge. All authority has been given to Me in heaven and on earth."

Jesus is the one who saves. God knows the heart of every person, and I think we need to let our Lord do His work according to His plan. We need to just follow and obey. Let God be God. Not everything is black or white. I do know that sin hinders the work of the Holy Spirit, and when we choose to sin we are choosing self over the Lord: Being a disciple of Christ means choosing Christ and living life to its fullest.

The first Scripture that the Lord gave me was 1 Peter 1, and the second was Ephesians 5, which I was told to read and reflect on every day. My third Scripture was John 13 followed by a command: "Wash the feet of many in the city of many." When I asked "Where?" the Lord said: "In the heart of the city." I was looking for a place until a friend of a friend invited us to see the band, "The Heart of the City." This is when I washed the feet of many in the city of many, and the rest is history. But my first command of action was to wash people's feet. This was just the beginning of what the Lord had for me. His first command of action for me was (and still is) learning to be a servant, learning to submit to others.

The Lord just gave me Revelation 7, John 14, and 1 Thessalonians 1:3. Faith produces action, and the Holy Spirit is the one who can give us this. We are not only here to be saved; we are here to love and connect to our living Lord and to the rest of His body. "Love the Lord with all your heart and with all your soul and with all your mind – and love your neighbor as yourself." The truest blessing is being connected to Christ; all the other blessings are just added to this.

There is no greater love than giving your life to the Lord. One word keeps coming to me over and over and that is *fortitude* so I will keep moving forward. Every day I ask the Lord for His help and I ask for His heart.

Revealing His heart,
Phoebe

Hi Greg,

This past week I have been contemplating the seven deadly sins. I was told that any sins cause much decay in the Spirit, and I am to recognize these sins. I was also told that whenever there is a conflict there is a spirit of pride. Even if the conflict is about misunderstanding or miscommunication, all can be resolved with a spirit of humility. And all these sins I was told can cause much damage to the physical body.

I also need to stress that there is much we have to take into consideration when we speak of God. There is another element to God that we all must have and it is reverential fear. It's not a fear that we understand in the secular term but a fear because of His holiness and majesty; it's an awe of His wonders, beauty, and creation. For this we must know that God is God and we are not.

When I contemplate who I am in Christ and my existence around me – I really have this peace and contentment. I know that when I am cold, lonely, or naked I have everything I need in Christ. Even on my deathbed I will honestly be able to say that I have everything I need in Christ. He is my all-in-all.

John 14, Philippians 2

In Him,
Phoebe

Hi Greg,

I just learned that someone in my family committed suicide. When something like this happens it makes me want to do more to reach out to the hurting and the lost. Jesus gives us truth and life.

Jesus served out of humility and obedience even to the point of death. God not only desires us to be His servant or friend, He desires us to be His lover and vice versa. This was a learning process for me. Now we are spiritual lovers. A spiritual lover is one who becomes intimate with the Lord and is willing to continually give his heart to Him no matter what the circumstance involves. He told me that many come to Him as servants and friends but very few come to Him in an intimate way. Every time I ask for Jesus' heart, He asks for mine.

The Lord told me that the most unrecognizable sin is pride, and this sin causes the most harm. Pride is what wrecks relationships. Pride tells us that we don't need help; pride blinds us to the truth; pride causes disunity. The Lord wants us to recognize this sin as well as others so that we can repent. The Lord is trying to prepare us.

Looking back on how God has used me is a miracle in itself. When God told me that He was going to make me an example to His church, I **believed** Him. At that time I didn't understand how or why but now I do. Jesus is our perfect example. All things are possible when we let go of our reasoning (conditions) and hold onto the Word of God. "Faith comes by hearing and hearing by the Word of God."

I try not to conform to rules or regulations (doctrines) because it restricts my mind and heart from doing what is more important, and that is to love. Love supersedes law. Sometimes the Lord tells me when I am motivated out of greed. He lets me know this and tells me to examine what I am doing. Whatever I do I need to do it out of love or else it's not worth doing. It is a change of attitude – a change of heart. He tells me to change my attitude by turning it around. It's not about what I'm going to get it's about what I am going to give – this establishes a change of heart.

I've noticed something happening more and more. God seems to be using women more now than in the past. I asked the Lord why and He said that men always deprived women of His power in the past, but now all that is going to change – even in children. (All are one in Christ.) I cringe when I hear leaders of the church express that God uses ordinary people. Are we not all ordinary without Christ? It is by God's Holy Spirit that we become extraordinary. One more thing that I would like to add – churches need to broaden their horizons. Whatever God is doing it is not about one church it is about His church as a whole. He wants unity within His body. Years ago God told me that John 17 was my mission. John 17 is His heart. Colossians 4:6 (NIV): "Let all conversation be full of grace and seasoned with salt so that you will know how to answer everyone."

Colossians 1, John 17, Hebrews 4:12

In Him,
Phoebe

P.S. I had a vision last night in which I saw a little lamb lying all alone in a corner. This lamb couldn't move. He looked perfect on the outside, but something was holding him back. I then saw Jesus gently pick him up and carry him to the light. I felt that this lamb was so weak, so confused, so hurt, and so full of pain, and Jesus came to him so that He could take care of the lamb and comfort him. But mostly Jesus wanted to take him home. My family member is fine—he is with Jesus now, and the rest of my family can take comfort in knowing that.

Jesus is the same yesterday, today, and forever. His love endures forever. Saturday night as I was falling asleep I heard, "Suffer for righteousness." Then I heard it from you on Sunday. I am going to keep giving hope to the hopeless through Jesus Christ our Lord and Savior. May the God of love and peace be with you.

Hi Greg,

The Lord told me that He wants you to be a lighthouse. He chose you to be a guide for light and truth. He keeps showing me this vision of a lighthouse, and He told me that is what He wanted for you and WHC. Now I am starting to understand where He is taking us. The question is do you want to accept this mission? I believe the church I used to attend could have had this mission guided by our Lord and Creator, but they chose otherwise (there is an irony to this). We all have choices in this world, and when we are given a mission from our Lord we have a choice to accept, believe, and receive it or decline and have it our own way. Belief is faith in action. The most freeing decision I chose was to let God come into my life and take over. Knowing that He is in control is very freeing.

Acts 18:9-10, John 8:12

The other day my son Blake (ten) came up to me and said, "Mom, do you know that I can hear God?" I asked him what He said and Blake replied, "God wants me to be a minister and build His house. Do you know what His house is? His house is His church." He paused for a while and then said, "Mom, where am I going to get the money to do this?" I told him that when God puts a seed in your heart He provides all that you will need when you believe. I went on to tell him that people can become His church (holy temple) and that he can start building now.

The Lord has recently warned me about the enemy: "The enemy is trying to steal your faith, so be on guard for there will be many wolves that come in sheep's clothing." I know the enemy loves to mock Jesus, but when the enemy interrupts me my faith increases all the more. Ephesians 6:12 (NIV): "For the struggle is not against flesh and blood it is against the rulers and principalities of this world."

Jesus is our river of life, and we all can draw everything we need from Him.

Peter 1:4, Revelations 12:11, Philippians 3

In His love,
Phoebe

Hi Greg,

This past week was such a beautiful time with the Lord, and so many unexplained events happened – all good things come from above. Here are some of the verses He gave me:

- "My church has to be cleansed by the Word of truth."

- "My church has to be Christ-centered."

- "Those who are foolish are wise and those who are wise are foolish; it is because you are secure in Me that you are wise."

- "In Christ alone can you be made whole."

- "It is by the power of My blood that you are saved."

About two weeks ago I had another dream: I saw the Lord standing high on a cliff. I looked up to Him and I wanted to be with Him, so I climbed as far as I could. I couldn't climb anymore so I just stood mesmerized by His beauty, and before I could say anything Jesus looked down at me. He knew that I had climbed as high as I could so He came down to me. As He stood before me Jesus didn't say anything. We just looked into each other's eyes and both knew what the other was thinking. He knew the deepest part of my soul, and I felt so united with Him that we became one. So many things were communicated that I know whatever happens from this day forward Jesus is my loving Guide. Our spirits are one.

As the dream was ending He said, "Phoebe, teach My children." And then I woke up, but I woke with a feeling of commitment and excitement. What makes this dream so odd is that when I went running the other morning I came to a cliff just like the one in my dream.

If you don't know by now I am very insecure without Christ. In August 2004 I was praying one day and asked God for His help. As I was praying I made a request to God. I asked Him to give me a sign of His promise that He would never leave me or forsake me. I asked Him to send me a rainbow of His promise to me. Sure enough about half an hour later it rained for twenty minutes, and afterwards a big bright beautiful rainbow appeared. After I marveled at the rainbow I heard: "And this is all you think I can do?" There is so much more that I haven't revealed, but just know that in God all things are possible. Get rid of the doubt that gnaws at your head.

Proverbs 15:33, 1 Peter 1:3, Matthew 22

Enjoying Him,
Phoebe

Hi Greg,

What is so ironic is that we are still struggling with the battle of Ai metaphorically. In the Old Testament (Joshua 7 & 8), Joshua learned right standing with the Lord. Personally and collectively we as the church need to learn from Joshua's battles. The Lord told me to keep everything simple so that all can learn. Ever since the Lord has shown me many truths my view has changed. I no longer care what a person has on the outside (i.e. strength, title, good looks). I care and get excited when the person is on fire for God. I also care for all those who don't know Him yet. My priorities have changed because it is no longer what I see that matters; it is what I experience from our Lord that truly matters.

The Lord also warns me of people and will tell me to pray for whatever their struggles are. I put my trust in Him because He sees the bigger picture. No matter what the circumstances may look like, the Lord is trustworthy. As I mentioned earlier, I work with people who are either mentally unstable or physically disable but all are suffering to some degree. I pray for these people, and why God doesn't heal them I don't know. There has been so much tragedy but my prayers never waver. I have to remember that God is God and I am not. God didn't heal every person Mother Teresa came into contact with, but He worked His mighty powers through her with all the people she encountered.

About a week ago I had a vision of thousands of sunflowers. I saw the sun move, and wherever the sun moved the sunflowers moved towards the energy of the sun (another metaphor). A couple of days ago I had a disturbing vision. I saw many people getting slaughtered. It was very dark and many people were getting killed. Right after that vision I had another one: Jesus came walking into a room where many people were gathered, and they were all glowing and wearing white robes, praising and adoring Him – it was like a big party.

Today I kept hearing Ephesians 5:16. The Lord said that this one is for the leaders of His church. He is preparing us, and I am praying that I will be with the Lord before evil takes place. He is communing with me on a daily basis. Just know that He wants all to come to Him so that we can share in this beautiful relationship with Him – He is longing for this. The Lord told me that building a bridge is good but crossing over is better.

Have a great day – this is the day that the Lord has made.

Matthew 12, Romans 12:1, 1 Corinthians 13:1, Ephesians 5:16

Trusting in His guidance,
Phoebe

Hi Greg,

The Lord took me out of an environment that hindered my spiritual growth and placed me in an environment that helps my spiritual growth. I am choosing my environment very carefully. Today I choose to be around people who are Christ-like because if I don't I know it will hinder my spiritual growth. The Holy Spirit edifies and builds up; He doesn't tear down. If there is a conviction of sin let the conviction come from the Holy Spirit not a self-righteous man. When a person demeans or condemns another he has a callused heart and is not hearing from the Holy Spirit. When a person has a hard heart they are not only dangerous to themselves, they are dangerous to those around them.

Do not let your heart be guided by your own choices; let the Lord guide you and you will enjoy the fruits of His Spirit—not the fruits of anger, doubt, distortion, condemnation, accusation, and lies. A prideful heart leads to doubt, and doubt leads to a wayward heart. Jesus did not bring doubt into this world He brought faith. God speaks to the humble. Whenever I start to judge another I always hear: "Take the log out of your own eye." This keeps me from falling into that trap. I thank God for reminding me of this. The Lord watches how we treat one another. The closer you are to God the less you want to sin – sin becomes very ugly.

It is easy to see when one preaches the Word of God from the head and not the heart of God. I put my hope and trust in God. Above all else we must love and pray for one another. When you put God first in your life all things change – love becomes the motivating factor.

1 Corinthians 13:1, Galatians 5

Five years ago when I was told to wash the feet of many in the city I was told that Jesus would be there. Our Lord is in the hearts of people no matter the color of their skin, their gender, or their age. When the Holy Spirit started working in my life it wasn't easy. I was like a child learning about God in a new truthful way. I had to let go of all the teaching from religious leaders and learn the truth solely from Him. It was like boot camp – I had to let go and listen and obey only Him. The first year was all about knowing the Lord and being obedient.

The other morning the Lord awakened me and asked: "What's in your heart? What is your deepest desire?" My response was: "I would love to see all people come to know You on an intimate level. I would love to see people free from the bondage of sin. I would love to see all Your people come together to build an army against the evil forces that rule this world. My deepest desire is that all would know You more so that this world can change through the power of Your Holy Spirit." None of this can be done unless we put our trust in our Lord and let Him lead and guide us by the power of His Holy Spirit.

Three visions: I saw numerous stars in the sky, each one unique in its own right, and then right after that I saw one bright shiny star bigger and brighter than all the others (Jesus). A couple of days later I saw a vision of you (Greg) typing away at your computer and letting the Holy Spirit do His work. His thoughts and words were flowing through you as you typed. The Lord is always transforming us into His likeness. There are areas in my life that He is purifying. This is a continuing process as I am not perfect – none of us is perfect, and that is why we have to seek Him and rely on His Holy Spirit to help us every day. Do not let anyone fool you – all have sinned and fallen short of the glory of God. It is by His grace that we are saved. We must daily humble our heart and know our Lord on an intimate level. Our life will never be the same.

God bless you and Merry Christmas!

Ephesians 2:10 (NIV): "For we are God's handiwork, created in Christ Jesus to do good works, which God prepared in advance for us to do."

In Him,
Phoebe

Hi Greg,

I was complaining about a certain person to our Lord and He said, "Phoebe, I love him as much as I love you. Learn to understand him and allow for mercy and grace." The Lord gave me this picture. He had all prophets, teachers, preachers, healers, encouragers, helpers, servers, evangelists, etc., together standing in a circle hand-in-hand, and Jesus was in the center of this circle. This is a picture of His body being connected and all having equal parts. Not one is more important than the other – it is more important that they're all connected. This is when the body is at its fullness – when they're all connected (1 Corinthians 12-14). He also gave me a simple yet beautiful vision and said: "Whenever you are suffering think of Me."

The other day I had to ask the Lord why I am bothered by people laughing at me. He ran this scenery through my head: I was in the eighth grade and on the B-squad football cheerleading team. I was a football and wrestling cheerleader throughout my junior and senior years, but my first year I was a pile of nerves. This scenery took place during a pep-fest for homecoming, and the whole school was there – all the junior and senior high school kids. I performed well until the last cheer. To make a long story short I messed up and everybody in the school laughed at me. I felt so humiliated that I went in a corner and cried. Some of my friends came and consoled me, but it didn't do any good at that time.

Ever since then I've had this thorn in my side about being humiliated. This is why I had a hard time standing up in front of people. Now it all makes sense to me. It's funny how I forgot about this, yet it is still stored in my memory. I don't need to prove my worth to anyone, but I needed this to understand why I choose to do certain things and why I like being behind the scenes. Well, not anymore. Ever since I had that special time with the Lord I have become much more confident. I have inner peace, inner resistance, inner strength, inner confidence, and inner joy – all connected to our Savior. I can't tell you how or what has happened to me, but for some reason I know that no one can shake my faith. This is what I have been teaching my children. No matter what people say about you just remember that you need to get the truth from God. Always look to God for answers and let no one steal your faith.

On Wednesday the Lord spoke to me in the early morning and told me that He is going to use me to bring in His kingdom. Of course I asked "How?" He said, "Wait and see." I know Jesus said that our bodies are the temples of God and the kingdom of heaven is inside us – but I don't understand. Again, I am going to let His will be done. Some of us have taken the blue pill and some of us have taken the red pill: Let's see how deep this rabbit hole goes - from the movie *Matrix*. Don't fault those who have chosen to remain in the comfort zone – their understanding will remain at this level, a level of worldly knowledge. This is why some of us are chosen to bring light to the truth. God loves us all the same, and not one of us is more important than the other; it is that we realize we can draw strengths from each other and work together in wholeness so that we can bring in His glorious kingdom.

1 Thessalonians 5, 1 John 4, Isaiah 9, Psalm 27

God bless,
Phoebe

Hi Greg,

I had three visions these past two weeks, and one awful dream. In the first vision I saw Jesus coming to this woman who was crying. He sat down next to her and let the woman cry on His shoulder. Jesus didn't say anything; He just let her cry, and then I heard: "Demonstrate My love towards others." God wants us to demonstrate His love towards others in this way, and this is how one can evangelize. An evangelist or missionary is just being like Christ wherever you are. We can talk all we want but God wants us to sincerely love others by our actions – this is what changes the heart. In the next vision I saw Jesus walking among a crowd of people, and many did not know Him. In the third vision I saw Jesus coming in the clouds.

Now, I had this dream about a certain individual, and in the dream I was talking to him. Every time I talked, this individual would puff up and become more prideful. The Lord wanted me to know that this was happening. When men start to idolize themselves it tells me they become lovers of themselves, and we know what the Lord says about this. Pride is blinding – those who are in pride only become more arrogant. I for one am attracted to humility and repulsed by pride. The Lord says that His Spirit is the Spirit of humility, and those who have the spirit of pride rely on their own human strength – beware. Ascertain the spirit of humility so that the Lord can do wonders through you.

A long time ago I made this promise: I told the Lord that I would serve Him the best I could. I promised that I would not interfere with the Holy Spirit's work. Therefore I set up boundaries for myself. I send the message and pray that the Holy Spirit will do His work. I then have to trust God that His message will reach people's hearts and transform them. God is interested in a heart change. Our Lord told me that if we really want to humble ourselves we have to give our hearts over to Him. This is the first step—being willing to let our Lord change our heart. We can preach all we want to, but it takes a choice and commitment to let Him change our heart.

I hold myself accountable to the Lord in all I do. Even if I have a "feeling" about something good, bad, or indifferent I turn it over to the Lord. We are beings with feelings, and we cannot discredit how we feel. The closer I am to the Lord the more genuine love I have towards other. If I feel a little uncomfortable around someone I will ask the Lord for discernment. Do not discredit a feeling; give it to the Lord. Let the Lord help you with everything you are.

Jesus came to seek and to save the lost; we as the body of Christ should do more seeking.

Isaiah 6, 1 Thessalonians 5, Revelation 2, Revelation 3, 1 John 5:21, 1 John 5

For His glory,
Phoebe

Hi Greg,

Do you remember the time I attended a WHC covenant meeting? As the leaders were talking I started crying. The reason for this was because right before the meeting as I was driving to church I was yelling at God, expressing my feelings to Him about His church. I told Him that I hated His church. I said I felt that His church represented a group of business organizations and all these organizations had an agenda that were not of God but only for business purposes. I told Him that I felt He was sending me on this rat race, and placing John 17 in my heart would only allow me to be disappointed again. I thought I would never enter a church that represented Jesus' heart. I thought that His church could do so much better if each church would lay down their differences and work together hand-in-hand – then the world would know the Lord by our love.

I am real with the Lord because He is real with me, and I told Him to send me to any church that represents His heart as He preached in John 17. I remember going to this covenant meeting and Paul Eddy was talking about how WHC tries to reach out to other churches. I started crying because I felt awful about yelling at the Lord. I then knew why I was at WHC. Well, I still have my struggles sometimes.

We can truly see and experience His kingdom by connecting to Him. The Lord not only came to save us He came to live in us so that we can share in His glorious kingdom, and to live life more abundantly. Life is worth celebrating. Celebrate who Christ is and who you are in Christ, and then you will know what the celebration is all about.

Ezekiel 33, John 14, John 3:3

Shalom,
Phoebe

Hi Greg,

As believers, our focus needs to be on Jesus and not on our disagreements. When people say that we should agree only on the Word of God, well, why are there so many different interpretations of His Word? There are so many disagreements between Christian denominations. We can have our disagreements and our different doctrines, but let's not destroy His church by attacking His body. I look at Christian churches like a marriage. In a marriage spouses can have their differences, but they choose to love and honor the Lord first, and then they love and honor each other. A marriage that puts Christ first and the spouse second is a strong marriage.

The same goes for the Christian churches; each one functions differently but each church should love and honor the other in Christ. And when our churches become strong we can then minister to those all around us. Just think how many we could reach if we would come together and start building His kingdom to those who are desperately in need of a Savior. What would this world look like if we could reach all those who are lost? Repentance is part of my daily walk.

I was told that my circumstances will get more difficult before they get better – I wouldn't expect anything less. Our Lord said that in this world there will be trouble, but take heart for our Lord overcame the world. One can pick and choose and attack and bruise – just like they did to Christ. Jesus did so much good with His ministry, but people chose to see things another way.

Hebrews 4

In Christ,
Phoebe

Hi Greg,

Last week I was telling my husband that when a Christian church starts to gain political power it becomes more destructive to God's kingdom. His leaders should stay on task of preaching His Word, not meshing their views with His Word according to their political gain. The Lord is not about force or coercion; He is all about living the life of love. When one knows the Lord he or she will not need to force any agenda other than preaching the Good News. When one matures spiritually, he or she will gain His wisdom and start living differently. (He always tells me to have a quiet spirit.) There is a right way and a wrong way of doing things, and then there is His way of doing things – I choose Christ.

The way I see it, we can have our different views but these views should be gained from the Holy Spirit, who then magnifies His beauty, not intensifies hatred. I have seen too much hate and ungodliness come from Christian people who think their way is right. When one takes an extreme view it just displays that that person is feeding the flesh. I have a close relationship with the Lord, and the Lord that I serve governs with love and peace – not to feed the flesh. Feeding the flesh is just walking in pride. Again, seek Him first and let Him dictate to your heart because by doing so you will see His kingdom flourish. His way is always the right way. His way always bears good fruit.

(The Lord reminded me to have a simple childlike quality because if I don't people may feel threatened or think I am being manipulative.) So let us treat one another with respect and not do any more harm to His body by destroying His parts. I pray that His believers will put Him first so that His body can come together in unity – that is a goal we must claim because this will advance His kingdom.

Romans 16, Ezekiel 2, 1 Thessalonians 2

Remaining in Him,
Phoebe

Hi Greg,

God is a God of promises, and when He promises He doesn't go against what He has promised; when man comes against His promises that man becomes a deceiver and is not to be trusted. I can relate to how Jesus went up against so many high priests because these high priests stood tall with their righteous indignation and accusation. These religious leaders were purposely trying to discredit Jesus and His work. But Jesus' wisdom was not of this world, and He put these people in their place. We know what

Jesus called them: "blind guides." The Lord told the Pharisees and Sadducees that the prostitutes and criminals will enter the kingdom of heaven before the self-righteous.

There are many legalistic, hypocritical church leaders that do not have the full knowledge of God's grace. Jesus always called out the righteous leaders on this. The religious leaders were always consumed with rules and never with knowing the heart of God. A perfectionist is an idolater. Division is set forth from this type of idolater. The Lord told me that those in leadership over His church who use condemnation as force will be judged. Those who try to discredit a brother or sister in Christ will be judged.

The Lord wants us to encourage and exhort one another in Him, not with judgment but with discernment. He is the righteous judge, and whenever a person takes His role he is playing God. Those who think they are righteous are not. And anyone who thinks they are always right is deceiving themselves. Not one of us is perfect, and the Lord knows He is still ironing out some things in my life, but I look to see how far I have come. That is a spirit of humility not pride. Pride looks at others and sees their sins as unworthiness, yet they have a log in their own eye.

With the Lord's help I will take a stand against anyone who mocks and creates dissension against the work of the Holy Spirit. Those who are doing this are walking in the spirit of pride and the spirit of judgment – they are playing the role of God. Live a life of worthiness not opposition.

God doesn't call the qualified; He qualifies the call. What I do in my head matters to the Lord. I try to keep myself humble, and whenever I step out of humility it affects people around me. I am a sinner who is in need of a Savior at all times. When one steps into pride he or she opens the door to the enemy and becomes the righteous judge: The enemy always tries to disqualify the call by using divisive tactics. Recognize his fruit and do not let him have a foothold. We all need to keep ourselves humble, and we need each other to do this. Take off the chains that Satan wants to weigh you down with, and break free from all his tactics. We are in Christ and have His authority to break free from anything that weighs us down.

1 John 5:4, 1 Corinthians 15:58, Matthew 16

In Him,
Phoebe

Hi Greg,

You know what is so freeing? It is the freedom to choose Christ and not be addicted to anything that this world has to offer. I am learning to live my life in balance and be free from guilt – guilt that comes from man not God. God does convict me of choices I make that are not aligned with His will because He wants me to stay on course, but it is done in such a way that I know I can change, and I don't have this guilt that creates heaviness which prevents me from moving forward. He also warns me of people.

About three weeks ago the Lord told me there are people who will try to eliminate me from this race I am on. He told me that whoever tries to eliminate me will carry an evil heart. He reminds me to stay on course and not look to my left or right; I must fix my eyes on Him. He told me that His promises are just and true, and (again) I am not to let anyone create doubt in my mind.

Do you know what I am praying for? Of course it is relevant to John 17 – I am praying that His body will become His body. Too many times I hear churches separated by religion, and religion is just manmade. I honestly wish that all believers would have the church entitled "The Body of Christ." All bodies joined together working differently but for the same goal. When we title His church with a specific religion we are creating division instead of unity – His body is disjointed. Again, we can have our difference but not idolize religion in the process.

About a month ago I had this dream, and now I see the same dream in recurring visions: I was standing on earth and the heavens opened up and came down upon me, and when this happened both the earth and I were transformed. It is hard to explain this vision, but the earth looked grungy and dirty, and when the new heaven came down upon this world earth became beautiful, bright, and colorful. Earth looked so radiant, and so did I. This is what we can expect for our future. I don't know when this will happen, but the Lord always delivers His promises.

I compare my faith to Abraham's. The Old Testament explains how Abraham always believed in God's promises and nothing shook his faith. I won't let anyone steal my faith in God. God's promises are just and true. I am so glad that people believe God is using me for His purposes – God wants to use all who are willing. I will remain in His humility and have a quiet and obedient heart. The Lord told me that He chose me because I am transparent and that I share His heart. What you see is what you get with me. I don't have to hide anything I do because God knows and loves me in all I do. Yes, sin leads to death, but when a person chooses Christ and has His heart the less sin there is in his or her life. God reminds me that love covers a multitude of sins. I am here to serve the Lord as well as others, and I hope and pray that these writings help to do just that.

Investing in His kingdom has more merit than investing in anything in this world. Last Saturday the Lord gave me Ezekiel 37 and told me that He wants to breathe His Spirit into all those who open their heart to Him – He showed me people in leadership.

Romans 15, Psalm 33, Psalm 92, Matthew 9, Hebrews 6, and Ephesians 3 (especially v. 10)

In Christ's love,
Phoebe

Hi Greg,

I was at a wedding last weekend and witnessed how the flesh can be deceived. The preacher talked about John 2 and how we should always listen to Jesus and take the example of Mary (his mother) who said to Jesus' servant: "Do whatever he tells you." The ceremony was beautiful until the preacher wrecked it by saying that man has the authority in the home. My spirit silently said "no." The Holy Spirit always tells me that God and God alone has the authority in a marriage. I have always said, "Do not let anyone define who you are but Christ: Do not let anyone define who you are by gender, race, creed, age, or any earthly status."

I have to take this time now to write about this subject because there are too many male leaders in His church who disqualify women and the roles God has given them. I am very passionate about women and their roles in the church and marriages. Women have been held captive in subordination by men for too long, and I am at liberty under the guidance of Jesus Christ to express my concern about men who speak with domination and authority. If these leaders would read the Bible and find out how women were used by our Lord, they would start to understand Him. The women God placed in the Bible were all under His authority. I have never interpreted that women should come under man's authority – Ephesians 5 was written in an era when women were thought of as property. And we know that Paul instructed Timothy in this era.

I have been given the authority to speak about this subject so that men can no longer have authority over women. I was told that my authority is in submission to the Lord, and He said that whenever He places someone in authority it is always in submission to Him. When man started taking over the "religious sect" of Christianity it actually damaged what Jesus did when He walked the earth. Now, look at our era and let's see where man has taken over and ruled. Can you not see that the flesh has been actively working in His church and not the Holy Spirit? Galatians 3:28 (NIV): "There are no longer Jews or Gentiles, male or female...all are one in Christ."

Yes, our Lord wants order and order will come when we are listening to the Holy Spirit. God wants the authority; He has seen what man does with authority and He wants all to let go of their flesh and come to Him in obedience. I have encountered more men who live in darkness (flesh) than light (Spirit) when it comes to this subject. The Lord wants all marriages to come together as one so that the couple can complete each other. The Bible doesn't say that a marriage means one is over the other. In a marriage one person is never over the other, and when a man tries to rule over the female partner he is not operating from the Spirit. The best illustration for a godly marriage is the triangle—with Christ at the uppermost point.

The Lord wants me to respect my husband and for him to respect me. The Lord wants me to come under my husband as much as my husband comes under me. Jesus came under people to the point of giving His life. I talked to my husband and my group about this subject, and my husband said that our marriage is very strong because we have love and respect for one another, and where he is weak I am strong and where I am weak he is strong.

We both draw strength from the Lord and we see Christ in each other. When a couple comes to realize that a marriage is a union that serves with sacrifice their union replicates Christ and His church. A divorce usually happens when one party starts living for self—this is what the church is doing today when men do not put women on an equal status.

This subject bothers me so much because the women in the church are predominantly held as second-class citizens. I want to see more and more women rise up just as the women did in the Bible and come under the authority of Christ not man. Jesus told me that He is the one who has the authority in our marriage, and we should always put Him first. Isn't it funny how man's interpretation has him first and God second? One who claims they should have the authority in a marriage does not know Christ. One who claims that a marriage is between a man and a woman and puts Christ as the authority in the relationship has the Holy Spirit working in them; anything else is just the flesh working and feeding itself. Jesus came in humility to serve others, and He wants us to do the same.

The Lord told me that our biggest deception is that we do not know the truth about who God is and about who we are in Christ. He said the enemy tries to keep us focused on ourselves so that we do not rely on God. The enemy wants us to live in the flesh and live out of the flesh. The enemy wants us to focus on ourselves so that the fruits of the flesh will operate instead of the fruit of the Spirit. Live in Christ, live for Christ, be a new creation. The one thing that matters to the Lord is that we all put our hope in Him and live for Him. "Whatever you do for the least of these you do for Me."

Philippians 2:16-17, 2 Timothy 2:7, 2 Timothy 2, Revelation 7:11, Matthew 7, Job 32, Psalm 112, Ezekiel 47:12

In Jack's memory,
Phoebe

Hi Greg,

The Lord is so awesome. I have been seeing miraculous changes and I know it is from Him. I may be in hardship but I see how God is operating to bring good out of this. Our God is so good all the time, and when I hear people say that evil happens because God allows it I have to freshen their understanding about who God is. Yes, God does allow evil but He is not the cause of evil. God has allowed us to have a free will so we are responsible for our choices. God is always drawing us to Him like a magnet, but because of our free will we have a choice to follow Him, follow the flesh, or follow evil. God does allow evil to exist in this world but we all have a free will to follow it or denounce it.

Many people have a deceptive picture of God, and our Father only wants us to choose Him because of His love for us—we love Him because He first loved us. How can people love God when they have a misconception about who He is? God wants us to be stewards of His Word, His truth, and we are not doing a good job of this. Unfortunately we like to do our own thing because of our flesh. God does not force us to do anything, so when someone robs me it wasn't a directive from God; it was because that individual lives in a lie and doesn't realize they are being used as a pawn. God does not stop evil because we are the ones who created it, and to destroy evil one could conclude that God would have to destroy humanity. God does allow evil to occur by our choices, but we have a choice not to choose it or to be influenced by it. Choose Christ and live.

This brings me to another area: deceptive carnal preachers. There are too many of them in existence, and just listening to some of them gives me chills up my spine because they are taking the truth out of context. This morning our Lord told me that He is dividing the wheat from the chaff in His church. He told me that

He is using me as His mouthpiece to separate His church from the counterfeit. He will be giving me many of His truths, and these truths will start the process of separating the true disciples from the false. There are so many deceptive carnal preachers, and because of this our Lord wants us to know His true church— the church who replicates Jesus (Calvary) and not the flesh or otherwise. He told me that many men have abused this position, and before He returns He has to separate the people who follow Him from those who choose otherwise.

The Lord told me that His church has already been built but because of man's pride His true church is hard to distinguish. He wants us to build on what has already been established. He wants us to continue to build on His truth, but we must get His message out. His sheep hear His voice and the people who have His heart will listen. The Holy Spirit is testifying to all truth, and anyone who comes against what the Lord is doing is operating from the flesh. He told me that whenever I am persecuted I have to remember not to take it personally and that if anyone persecutes me they are really persecuting Him.

Jesus gave me a vision of a storm and told me that I should expect a storm because people have given into the flesh so much that they have a hard time distinguishing truth from lies. He told me that He will always be with me no matter what the storm looks like. Finally, He told me that He loves me more than I would ever know.

I seem to be stronger than before. Sometimes hardship brings courage and resiliency. I know that prayers are being answered, and I thank God for that. He is always working to bring good out of a mess. There is no other name above Jesus Christ. He is our all-in-all and the giver of life; anyone that tries to put any other name above our Lord is operating from the flesh, or something else.

The Lord told me there will be more evil upon the world and that He wants His children to unite. He said that His church would not be able to stand as it is right now. This evil that exists will allow His children to unite in love and allow the separation of the wheat from the chaff. He wants no one to perish, but He does allow each one of us to choose. He then gave me Revelation 7, and I have been hearing this Scripture ever since. He wants His church to unite so that it can be seen as it was originally intended. I can envision the true church uniting when His children focus on Him instead of their flesh.

1 John 2, 1 John 5, Psalm 20, Matthew 26:10, Proverbs 20

In Him,
Phoebe

Hi Greg,

I asked the Lord about baptism because I wanted to know if there was more to it, and He told me that baptism symbolizes that a person has chosen to give Him their heart – it is a public confession of faith. There is no higher calling than to choose the Lord. Choosing Christ starts the process of transformation. I asked the Lord why men are divided over the meaning of baptism. He told me it is because men make more decisions in pride than in humility, and when His children come together in humility you will see unity. Why don't we leave the semantics alone and focus on the desire to tell the truth to people. The Lord wants no one to perish; that is why He is sending out His message of truth. The Lord wants all to know Him and all to come to Him.

What happens to the ones who continue to live their life based on a lie? I don't know…I leave all that up to God. I do know that our

God is a loving God who knows the hearts of all people, and what decision God makes is His and His alone. I have a responsibility to get this message out to everyone who is willing to listen, and for those who do not…well, let's just leave that to God.

Let's put down our pride and live in humility so we can depend on God and His sovereignty. Let's be His people who live by His Spirit and not the flesh. I would like to see all the gossip, innuendoes, malicious remarks, and backbiting stop – these things tear the body of Christ. Die to the old way of life. I teach my children about the way of life. I teach my children about the enemy and his tactics and how he wants to pull us into anything that is against God. Sex, drugs, alcohol, and other worldly pleasures are the lies of the enemy because we deny the design and principles of God. I teach my children that they will be walking in the enemy's territory if these pleasures are taken out of context for which God originally designed them. Any pleasure can be an addiction, and if it is out of God's design each person will experience pain, hurt, disappointments, instability, etc.—not to mention the mental, physical, spiritual, and emotional diseases that could infiltrate the mind and heart of anyone willing to get sucked in.

What God teaches is that we choose Him first before anything in this world. God wants us to choose Him because we love Him, and when you have this principle you will find joy. His joy is fulfilling and complete. We live in a world that offers many things that could destroy our relationship with God. I look back at my journey and see how wrong legalistic teaching is. When I see a legalistic pastor teaching about hell and damnation out of context, I want to tell him to step down from the pulpit. Jesus let the prostitutes and tax collectors into heaven before the legalistic leaders.

I am here to love as God does and teach and demonstrate His love. Yes, there is a hell, but it is not up to me to put people there – I refuse to play God's role. Any pastor who has a legalistic standpoint on this, please turn from the flesh or step down from the pulpit – that is integrity.

You know what is so ironic? My brother loves the Lord but he doesn't like the church's teaching. He has experienced so much shame and guilt that led right to hell from Christian teaching – that did more damage to him. The truth is that there are too many preachers teaching this way, and what does it do to a person? He or she will want to cling to something else. Please speak the truth in love and let God be God. I look back to where I started on this journey with our Lord, and a lot of progress has been made but there is still more that waits. Work together in humility to form a bond of peace; let that be your focus, for the Prince of Peace.

Two visions: I saw these men who looked like Middle Eastern leaders all standing around confused, and the Lord told me these men are in a fog. Another vision: I was with our Lord and I felt the power of His love, and it literally took my breath away. There are no words to describe this love. All I know is that it was a little glimpse of what is to come. I may never know the fullness of His love while I am in this physical body, but I do know that when I am with the Lord this love I felt will be magnified and it is truly powerful.

Jeremiah 3, Jeremiah 30, Isaiah 11, Philippians 4:13

In His reign,
Phoebe

Hi Greg,

Yes, we all will suffer for Christ but it is choosing His will over ours. As I tell my children, the suffering we incur when we choose the flesh does not gain anything but personal setbacks. Suffering for Christ is different from suffering for the flesh. When we suffer for Christ His kingdom grows, and when we choose to suffer for our fleshly appetites the enemy's kingdom grows. Whenever I suffer for Jesus I invite God in and change happens, and sometimes this change hurts – suffering can be seen as a teacher. I think suffering has too much negative connotation attached to it.

When we live in the bigger picture, suffering for Christ and for others can be an honor. When we suffer for Christ we are blessed. We must wake up to the difference of the two sufferings. It truly is a blessing to choose Christ and to suffer for His kingdom because when we do this our character grows into His likeness. God wants to burn away anything that does not resemble Christ, and sometimes it hurts.

Lately I've been struggling with so much doubt, and doubt creates an illusion. Whenever this happens I have to bring in the truth. A couple of days ago I had this dream in which I was talking to my friend. I was telling her not to worry about the enemy's power because we have the power of God in us. As soon as I told her this truth I was lifted up and thrown back against the wall. I was in shock as I could not see what I was up against. I was very frightened and lost the sense of reality until my friend kept telling me to say "Get behind me, Satan, in Jesus' name." And when I focused on what my friend was saying I recovered the confidence I have in Christ to speak the truth—and then I woke up.

That is just like what's happening now. I am up against a force, a prince of the power of the air, and I cannot see with fleshly eyes; I have to see with spiritual eyes. I can be taken by surprise at any time, but the point is that we need people in our lives to help us get through these rough times. When the enemy comes upon any of us and takes us by surprise, we need others who are in Christ to help us get back on our feet, to stand firm on the truth. I know there are times I think I don't need help from anyone, but the truth is that I do. I love it when I hear that people are praying for me; there is a sense of love, strength, and comfort. We need the Lord and we need one another. The Lord wants His body to grow with love for one another. We all have our struggles from time to time, and we need one another to gain strength and encouragement.

The Lord wants us to depend on Him for help. He also will send someone in His likeness to anyone who is struggling, and we need to recognize this. I teach my children to recognize the Spirit of God speaking in them and to them because they will be tempted by something in this life, and it is imperative that they recognize His voice of truth so they can overcome the temptation and defeat the enemy's tactics. I give the Lord all glory because without Him we all would be at the bottom of the pit, but because of His love we are a new creation.

Some people have not had the chance to choose Christ because they lack understanding about who God is, or they may not have heard the gospel, but let God decide the hearts of all and let us not play God but serve Him—love people to Christ. It is an honor and a privilege to do so.

I have so much confidence in the Lord that at times I cannot tell if it is confidence or pride, but the Lord told me that confidence is from Him and pride is from me. I need to keep drawing strength from the Lord, which builds my confidence.

The other day my nine-year-old asked me why God blinded Saul. She wanted to know if God would do this to her because of her sins. I went with it for a while and told her yep, and if you don't obey your parents…well, I couldn't leave it like that so I told her the truth. I told her about God's purpose, love, and restoration. The Lord is into restoration, and the message He wants me to send out to all is "turn your hearts back to Him."

I had a dream a while ago, and in this dream I was alone and the world was a very dark and evil place. People were dying to the left and right of me, and I was standing by myself speaking about God's love. A lot of evil people surrounded me, and when they heard me speak about God's love they all started to circle me as if they were going to kill me. In this dream I spoke boldly about God's unconditional love and told people to turn their hearts back to Him because it is never too late to do so. I remember having this rod and holding it up to heaven as I was preaching the Good News. And then I woke up. It's odd but in my spirit I don't have anxiety about what is going on in the world. I know that this is just a prelude to what is to come. The other day I kept hearing "Do not disparage the truth."

Disappointment comes because of the lack of understanding. When we develop a deeper relationship with our Lord the questions we have will change as well as our understanding to them. We need to rest in His presence and let Him be in control.

Two visions: I saw a healthy plant, and all of a sudden radiation hit it and the plant withered and died. In another vision I saw all these healthy cells in a Petri dish, but bacteria was moving fast in this dish attacking the healthy cells.

Matthew 7, Mark 10, 1 Thessalonians 3:9, 1 Thessalonians 3, Ephesians 2

In His everlasting love,
Phoebe

Hi Greg,

Last week while I was at the cabin the Lord told me what church reflects Sardis and what church reflects Smyrna. He said there will be some who oppose this message, but I am to remember that I'm just a messenger. He also told me that I am not supposed to worry about what people say about me because many are living a lie. When people slander me with accusations and lies it only affirms what I already know – attacks are from the enemy. He appointed us to build His church. The message I need to give you is quite clear: "People of God, humble your heart and give it to God. In doing so God can use every cell in your body." Listen, for the Lord is speaking to those who have the ears to hear…

This is why I am against any church that relies on the words of man and not on the Word of God. Man's opinion is just man's opinion. Too many times I hear men speaking from the pulpit without God's Spirit. When a person thinks they have all the answers and interpret the Bible without God's wisdom they just prove that they are operating from the flesh. We need to recognize any church living in darkness and pray for these churches because many are being deceived. God wants no one to perish, and He wants all to come to Him. It is important to pray against any divisive spirit. A spirit that is divisive is not of God.

When I gave my life to Jesus I told Him He could use me according to His purpose and that I am willing to do whatever it takes so more people would know Him. I told Him that I am willing to give my life for this. I told the Lord that I want Him to use my life as a testimony. After I prayed that prayer I could feel the Lord's power and presence, and it still remains.

Whatever I do, I do it for all who are willing to listen. I pray for His church, and I pray for His people. I pray that more leaders will enter a relationship with our Lord and become more and more like Him.

Our Lord doesn't choose anyone who is just a willing participate – He chooses those who have aligned their heart with His.

Ephesians 5, Jude, 1 Peter 5

Enjoying Him always,
Phoebe

Hi Greg,

Do you know how one can tell if a church leader is operating from the flesh? It is when he or she limits God's power and speaks about God's conditional love. The God I serve is a God of unlimited power and unconditional love. God's heart is to include all people. I used to attend a church that indoctrinated my thinking that God only saved a select few, and this church would give me points to establish who was in and who was out. I remember thinking that I had to change according to what they were preaching or I would not enter heaven. They claimed that God only accepted a clean heart; I guess no one is suited for heaven.

God continually transforms the hearts of those who have accepted the Lord as their Savior. He is always giving us indications that He wants us to have a personal relationship with Him, but we have to take the time to know who He is and understand how He operates. I refuse to put God in a box. I am so glad I sought the truth and became free from the bondage of legalism. I am praying for any church that is dead to Him.

Many churches claim Jesus as their Lord but their heart is not right. When one has Christ in his heart, he will start preaching with His wisdom and love. What did Paul say about love? If we do anything without love we are just like a clanging cymbal, and many churches today are operating without God's love and wisdom. It is easy to discern these churches. Jesus said, "You will know My disciples by their love." The Lord wants the leaders of His church to know His heart so that many followers will not be misled. He said His church has to change because His heart is for the lost, least, and hopeless. He also told me that His church is not prepared for His return because it is too divided. He wants His church to be a shelter for the lost and hurting. He wants His church to be united so that many people will experience His love.

People from the outside looking in just see many churches as organized religion. I am praying that His church will wake up and come together so that many more people will know the Lord. It is His church that can reach the lost, but too many are busy trying to prove they are right. I also told God that I am not equipped to build His church, and He reminded me that I am not the one who is doing the building – He is. He reminds me not to look at myself but to look at Him for all things. He is the only one who can save us.

The other night the Lord reprimanded me in His own gentle way. He told me there are different types of leaders in His church— some truly have His heart and others want to have a heart like His but don't know how to achieve this. Some leaders lead His church like a business and think they are doing Him a service. He told me not to judge or be too harsh on anyone because everyone is at a different level. He told me that I could turn many away from hearing His true message, and that is to have His heart. The Lord wants me to ask for forgiveness and tell anyone I hurt that I am very sorry. He said He knows I want to help people but that I am hurting many in the process. Please forgive my actions. After this experience I had tears in my eyes because the Lord allowed me to see and understand the hearts of many, and I have never felt closer to Him.

Philippians 2, James 3, James 3:15, Proverbs 21, John 3, and James 1:12

In God's tender heart,
Phoebe

Hi Greg,

Faith comes by hearing and faith comes by believing every Word of God. When Jesus speaks many will ask if it is literal or symbolic; it can be either or both. The point is let the Word speak to your heart and watch the mountains move. I asked the Lord why most preachers are not preaching on the Holy Spirit, and He told me to give it time. Knowing the Lord comes from reading His Word and letting His Spirit guide a believer into all truth. I want people to know our Lord because when the Lord takes over a life this life becomes evident of change and affects many others.

As you said the sum of all the parts equals the whole. Well, let's get these parts together and make the body whole and see how the body moves. The Lord will bless when we start seeking the needs of other members of His body; the Lord will bless those who multiply. Whatever the Lord asks from us is never something we can accomplish on our own. It is His principle for us to rely on Him for everything. When we rely on Him and seek Him first, He will always be there for us – He always comes to us as a friend. I am not interested in the politics of the church; I am only interested in the minds and hearts of each soul.

The Lord told me that He chose you to work with me because you honor women in the ministry. He said that because men blame Eve for making a choice to eat the forbidden fruit, many men hold this against women and do not trust women for this reason. The Lord wants His body whole and healthy, and He wants women to be trusted with His work and service. He told me that He was sent to reverse what was done in the garden. He laid down His life for all people who will receive Him, but pride has swept the majority of people and many are being led astray. I am here to remind people what the Lord has done for all of us—what He did on the cross. The veil was torn and the Lord wants reconciliation with all people, men, women, and children of all classes and races.

Philippians 2:19, Acts 2, Proverbs 1, Matthew 12

Unity in His body,
Phoebe

Hi Greg,

Here is another principle I am starting to understand. The more grace I offer to others the more grace is offered to me. When I extend mercy to others mercy is extended to me, and so on and so forth. The Lord told me that it is the same with unforgiveness. When I decide not to forgive someone He sees this and puts it in my heart to forgive that individual because He wants me to forgive others so that I can forgive myself; in doing so the cycle of unforgiveness is broken. But if I choose not to forgive, then the Lord will not forgive me for my part in this conflict until I release it to Him: "You reap what you sow."

We know that our Lord is faithful and just to forgive our sins but we have to release them to Him. The Lord can do all things through us if we let Him. We have to remember that He is in the business of saving grace, and we must look to Him for guidance and help for this throughout our lives. We all need to be open to the Lord's prompting because He wants restoration with all relationships.

Sometimes I have a hard time waiting on the Lord, and that is one of my weaknesses. When I want answers I want them as soon as yesterday. The Lord told me that when I want answers, I am supposed to come to Him because He is the expert. I just have to have patience and that is hard for me.

The Lord told me that when my heart is not open to hearing Him, His Spirit will come through my family members.

Lastly, He said that no one will know the hour or time for His return but everyone should prepare as if their life is depending on it. I keep hearing this passage: "No eye has seen or ear has heard, and no mind has imagined what God has prepared for those who love Him."

Romans 8, John 6, 2 Timothy 3:4, Revelation 3

In Him always,
Phoebe

Hi Greg,

The Lord has put something in my heart to share, and it is about the subject of money. He told me that many leaders of the church are influenced more by money than by our Lord. He warns that we all can start off serving the Lord with good intentions, but because of outside influences many people are dissuaded from serving Him. And money can start being a master to those who are not continually seeking God's wisdom; money is an outside influence that can damage a relationship.

If leaders start putting their trust and security in money then the church becomes just like any other secular business. We cannot serve two masters. The Lord wants leaders to pray for the body of Christ and trust in Him alone. Our God is a jealous God; He wants our hearts to be committed to Him and not influenced by money. The leader's job is to preach the Good News so that many will give Him their heart, and by doing so the world will know that Jesus is Lord. The message is quite clear: Trust in the Lord with all your heart and watch His blessings flow. Offer everything you have to Him, and let the Lord take care of the rest because He owns it all.

About three months ago the Lord told me to be more disciplined with money. I was lukewarm about this and obeyed some of the times. Over a month ago my husband went to a meeting at work, and they unanimously decided to pull a major product line. This resulted in Craig losing about one-third of his income. My husband came home that night and we all had a family meeting about our finances. We told the kids that we were on a tight budget for a while and had to make concessions. I became disciplined with money and solely trusted in the Lord, and He told me that if I maintain this discipline He will bless us with more than we ever thought.

Well, about a week ago Craig came home and told me that a person was retiring and Craig would get most of his accounts. And since they pulled this one product line it resulted in selling another product, which affects Craig's sales, and they will continue to skyrocket. Needless to say, the Lord came through but I didn't expect it to be so soon. Craig's income is back to normal, and in time he should make more money than we ever expected. Craig and I have many different investments, and we own more than we owe. We have it set up so that if anything were to happen to either of us, we could sell any one of our investments and pay off the house. We prefer to have a house payment so we have some tax advantage.

The principle here is that we need to listen and trust the Lord with everything. Again, the Lord doesn't want leaders running His church as if they are relying on the money. He wants this message to sink in loud and clear because many church leaders are running a business instead of leading an army for Christ. There is a war we must battle, and money influences and infiltrates the hearts of many. We need to be an example of His trust and beauty so that His glory is on display.

Matthew 18, Luke 19, Psalm 23, 55

Trusting in Him,
Phoebe

Hi Greg,

When I reflect on my past I have to admit I am grateful for the all my experiences with the Lord because growing in the Lord may hurt, but I am grateful to deepen my relationship with Jesus. God was always working behind the scenes helping me become wiser and stronger. "Please do not judge what you do not know for judgment comes from a misguided heart." This is what I received from the Lord, and He went on to say: "Leave all judgments to Me and be wise and encourage and help one another along the way."

I had another disturbing vision/dream when I went to bed on Monday night. I saw a mother running and kids screaming, and I kept seeing a picture of a knife – it was very disturbing. I remember looking at the clock at 1:30 a.m. That morning I woke up and went to my first client. She had the news on and they were describing a homicide/suicide that happened in Burnsville; this all took place around 1:30 in the morning. The vision/dream I had earlier that morning was on the news. The Lord told me to pray for the kids who witnessed this horrific act. Maybe someday I will meet them.

A couple of months ago my sister-in-law told me about an experience that happened to her brother. He kept getting these images about an electrical box at his church, and he didn't know why so he told the pastor and urged him to check the church's electrical box. When the pastor went to check the box he noticed something faulty, and the pastor knew if he didn't get it fixed it would have started a fire. I pray that more people will be open to His Spirit because it is these experiences that can change a person or event.

The more we are open to God the more we will notice Him. God is always working so I pray that we are willing to be more open to His every way. God wants to move on us like nothing before, individually and collectively.

1 Peter 1, Revelation 13, 2 Peter 2-3, 1 Corinthians 13

In His beauty,
Phoebe

Hi Greg,

If you want to see a change it starts with you. The Lord wants all people to have a personal relationship with Him, and this should be our main focus as the church. Reading His Word and spending time with our Lord will further deepen our relationship. When the leaders of the church are open to His guiding Holy Spirit, changes will occur. We should always seek the Lord first before we make any decision; remember that He has first place in our lives.

Coming to the Lord and repenting is the first step. The next step is developing a relationship with Jesus. Again, prayer, reading His Word, and listening to the Holy Spirit all lead to a personal connection with our Lord Jesus Christ and with other members of His body. There is no doubt that the church has to change and it starts with each individual who is leading His church.

It bothers me that the church does not teach people about their gifts. Every child of God has gifts, and we need to teach people about their individual gifts. When a church claims to be a Protestant church they seem to be under the umbrella of evangelizing, but there are other gifts that God has ordained besides evangelizing. Yes, it all leads to spreading the Good News, but the church is really missing the wholeness of Jesus' teaching. And then there are the Catholics who do so much service for our Lord but don't speak about developing a personal relationship with Him—too much religion does a disservice to our Lord.

The point is I don't care what religion a person claims, but claim Jesus first and let His Spirit guide His church, and let each individual claim the gifts that God has given him. The job of leaders is to come under people and help them develop what God intended for them. We always need to point to Jesus Christ.

I had a couple of visions. Last Sunday as I was sleeping I saw a massive fire coming at me. This fire kept getting bigger as it came toward me, yet I remained calm and didn't move. I stood my ground and felt this great authority from above, and I yelled

"Get back!" The fire moved back and then I woke up from my dream.

Luke 13, Ephesians 4, Ephesians 4:7, Matthew 25

In Him always,
Phoebe

Hi Greg,

We speak about tearing down walls between the Christian churches, but nothing is happening. The Lord gave me this wisdom: "In time everything will get better." Circumstances may not get better, but our joy is in our Lord. Whenever I am having a bad day I seek the Lord's wisdom first and then my family and close friends because they listen without judging and always tell me to remain focused on Christ – they become Christ to me.

Preachers are in an arena of great influence for our Lord—quit judging and remain faithful by always seeking wisdom from our Lord. And as always humility is a great place to be. We need to make our body a holy living sacrifice. We need to be filled with the Holy Spirit every day. Being filled with His Spirit simply means being connected and constantly submitting ourselves to our Lord moment by moment.

The Lord has explained to me what He meant by separating the wheat from the chaff. He told me that He wants to save people and not separate them. He told me that I am going to sift the truth from the lies in His church. He said that when preachers put limitations on other people, what they are really doing is limiting Him. Women have been oppressed in the churches for centuries, and it is time to release that demon. The church that exemplifies

Jesus is a church that operates from His Spirit. The Lord wants His church to look more like Him.

1 Peter 1, Romans 12, John 9:10, John 9, John 10, 1 Corinthians 3, 2 Timothy 3

Loving Him,
Phoebe

Hi Greg,

One thing I try to do is be Christ-centered. I look at every angle from His point of view and make most of my decisions in this way. I used to be very defensive whenever people would question me about anything I was doing. Now that I have a Christ-centered view, I look at every question as an opportunity to plant seeds for His kingdom. I realized that I don't have to defend my character because I let Christ who lives in me flourish.

I had a disturbing vision last night: I saw the Lord walking towards a pasture where there were many sheep. As He approached, the sheep didn't want to be bothered by Jesus and they all scattered. This vision bothers me because many people want a different kind of Jesus. Our Lord wants us to let Him in. He is standing at the door and waiting, but many people want to live their lives for themselves. You all want to live a beautiful life? Well, let the Lord in and let Him be your guiding light because there is nothing more beautiful than this.

Tuesday morning I had another disturbing dream and it had to do with me. As I drive to my job each day I do a lot of work "at the wheel" so that I can save time, but there have been many close calls. In this dream I was driving with one hand on the wheel as usual. As I was trying to write down what I was hearing from the caller,

I looked up and noticed a sharp curve approaching fast. When I realized I wasn't going to make that turn I panicked and turned the wheel very sharply, went across the median, and rolled my car several times – and then I woke up. This dream was a wake-up call and I am now changing how I drive. Oddly, this exact scenario happened to a woman in Burnsville the very next morning.

Daniel 5:17, 1 Corinthians 16, 2 Corinthian 5

In Him,
Phoebe

Hi Greg,

Has anyone ever said anything that rubbed you the wrong way? This has happened to me but sometimes these comments started to burn a passion in my soul so that I am on fire for God. Sometimes it takes friction to start a fire.

John 10

In His ways,
Phoebe

Hi Greg,

God is so good because He keeps on giving. However, when I signed up for this ministry I didn't know the supernatural dark forces were going to come at me with full force. Many unusual things were happening around me, and I couldn't explain any of it. The Lord is doing something beautiful in all of us, and if anyone corrupts or twists this, one has to know that it is not of God. He sees and knows all things – this is why I am dependent on Him. Trust and follow Him first because this will lead to freedom. If we put our hope in God we will see changes, changes in the heart. One thing I learned is that man is never satisfied, but God is. He has unconditional love for all of us and He sees the progress that has been made for His purposes first!

The Lord builds His church by allowing us to partner with Him, and He allows us the necessary qualification to do so such as the heart, energy, time, resources, and spiritual gifts—and all are influenced and motivated by love. And how does this happen? It is by a personal connection with Jesus Christ and knowing who you are in Him. Too many people limit God's church to a building – His church is much more than that: His church will replicate Jesus. Jesus wasn't stuck in a building; He spread His kingdom among people. So did Paul, Peter, and all of His apostles.

Many disadvantaged people cannot get out of their place of residence because of factors that limit them. These people cannot get to church on the weekend, so I bring church to them. When we start limiting God to a building we limit God. I don't serve a materialistic god I serve a God who is Spirit, truth, and love – I pray that my service always reflects His will. I have a peace that I can't explain but it is so beautiful.

1 Peter 1:3, Romans 11, 3 John, John 1:11, James 5, Luke 20

Walking in His peace,
Phoebe

Hi Greg,

When I signed up for this mission I knew I would be misunderstood from the beginning, but that is nothing compared to what Christ has done. Satan is always up to his old tricks, but I will continue to serve our Lord. When I write about my experiences with the Lord it doesn't mean that we all have to follow the same way; it simply reveals the Holy Spirit's work in my life. The Lord told me that I must be obedient to the call; He then told me to remain in Him. There are a thousand different mission fields, and feeding the poor is just one way to bring the hope of Christ to the world. God will put it on your heart where to spend your time, energy, gifts, and resources.

The other day I kept hearing the words "you have not because you ask not." Well, I am asking for help in this. Early one morning last week the Lord woke me up and gave me this vision: I was kneeling at His feet crying. He brought me up to standing position, looked me in the eye, and said, "Phoebe, I do not condemn you," and then the vision was over. Many people will condemn me because of the path I chose, but I will always remember this vision because it is the Lord I serve.

The Lord is our Bread of Life, and every day we need to bring forth this nourishment (His Word). Satan wanted to twist and minimize this with his first temptation to our Lord. His second twisted temptation was worship, and his third twisted temptation was to test God (testing brings doubt). Satan continually wants us to doubt the Father, Son, and Holy Spirit. What Jesus did on the cross nullifies all temptations. Satan continually tests us, but the Good News is waking up to the truth of who we are in Christ. When we finally wake up to this truth, these temptations no longer have an effect on the flesh. Die to self and live for Christ. Let all temptations die throughout the day so that you can move and breathe in Him.

God wants us to seek first His kingdom and His righteousness, and all these things will be given to us as well. When Jesus came to give life and give it abundantly, He also came to destroy the works of the devil. The Father, Son, and Holy Spirit are working together so that He will be magnified. Please let us work together to bring forth His glory on earth. Amen!

Merry Christmas,
Phoebe

Hi Greg,

I remember going to bed one night this week and feeling that I have failed our Lord because I have prayed and written about unity within His body and have yet to see this transpire. I also have spoken many times about women's roles as leaders within His body. The Lord knows my heart, and that is why He needed to remind me that condemnation is not from Him. Since then I decided to take a stand against any form of condemnation. The Lord wants me to speak the truth, pray about it, and then let it go. He doesn't want me to worry about anything because He is the one who is in control.

I am learning to present what the Lord has given me and live in His blessing, which is joy and peace. My joy and peace don't come from what the world gives – it comes from what the Lord gives and knowing that my eternal life is secure. So much has happened lately, and I really want to ponder on what the Lord instructed me to do. The Lord wants His church reformed because evil is going to become more intense, and more people will fall into deception. This is why the church needs to be a strong tower.

The Lord explained to me that it is the Seed of the woman who will crush Satan's head, and that the woman represents the church. He told me the Seed is His Word and that the church who lives by His Word will unite as one, and this church, along with Him, will crush the head of Satan; Jesus the **Word of God** will crush Satan. The church is His body and He is the Head. The Lord told me that the church has always been Satan's target because Satan wants no one to follow or submit to God. Anyone who claims the Lord Jesus Christ as their Savior is a walking testimony. Our temple is His body and the body is His church. The church represents God's heart. God wants obedience because He wants to destroy evil.

Again He reminds me that He will be separating the wheat from the chaff, and, yes, God will test the hearts of many. He told me that the spirit of the antichrist is in His church. He wants no one to perish, but He also knows there are some who have turned against Him. When I read Revelation it seems like we are losing the battle, but our testimony is what will defeat our enemy. We need to know and live for truth.

One night I was feeling insecure about all this, and I prayed for someone or something to help me understand this more. My small group helps but I need more. When I was praying Rick Joyner's name came to my mind. I went online to see if he had any current books available. I ordered the book *The Torch and the Sword*. After reading this book, it occurred to me that there are many similarities between what the author experienced and what I am experiencing—it's not a coincidence. I don't know where this is headed, but I do know that the Lord wants His people to follow Him. As an act of obedience, please listen to the Holy Spirit; He will be guiding your every step. Reformation will come from an obedient heart. We are His temple, we are His church, and we have a choice to make: are we going to live for ourselves or die to self and live for Christ? Ponder this question in your heart.

1 Thessalonians 4, 1 Timothy 3-4, Revelation 20-21,
2 Chronicles 3

In courage and strength,
Phoebe

Hi Greg,

It is His people, His body, His church who can reach the least and lost. Ephesians 6:12 (NIV) came to me again: "For our struggles are not against flesh and blood, but against the rulers, against the authorities, against the powers of the dark world and against the spiritual forces of evil in the heavenly realms. Therefore put on the full armor of God, so that when the day of evil comes, you may be able to stand your ground."

Looks like God wants our obedience more than sacrifice, but in our obedience to Him we are a living sacrifice: Jesus gave His life willingly. It is out of our love and obedience to the Lord that we may be asked to give our life as a living testimony, a living sacrifice. It may look like we're losing the battle, but we are not. We are not going to win evil by conquering with force; we are going to win evil by giving up our life out of love. Jesus said that we would be able to do more than He did. Well, let's destroy evil – even if we have to give our lives. The early church understood this concept, and here we are in this time to rebirth that truth. Have the mind of Christ, have a victor's mentality and not that of a victim. I know that persecution will come, and that is why I choose to live in His joy and peace – the living Word of God.

Jesus was always persecuted by the religious leaders of His time because they operated in pride. A person operating in humility does not accuse. Here is truth in humility: the world is influenced by the devil, and Jesus came to destroy his work—we are allowed to partake in this. The devil is trying to destroy God's work and God's people. The Sadducees and Pharisees thought they were right with God. When pride takes over a heart, that person has a misguided perception. A prideful heart takes on an ugly disposition. It's no wonder why the Lord wants His church to change. Pride keeps people away, and because of this more people have a skewed perception of God.

The church can take on the Lord's beauty or it can take on an ugly existence. We all need to change with this truth in mind: when someone slaps you on one cheek you offer the other. To become spiritually mature is to take no offense. Accusations do not come from God.

I had a vision about a month ago in which I was kneeling in full armor before the Lord. I held my helmet in my right hand under my left arm with my head bowed before our Lord. He took out this sword that looked like fire and tapped my head with it. I kept hearing Hebrews 4:12: "The Word of God is living and active. Sharper than any doubled-edged sword, it penetrates even to dividing soul and spirit, joint and marrow; it judges the thoughts and attitude of the heart."

In a dream last night I was standing alone in darkness, and I had this fiery sword. Whenever I used the sword it would penetrate through the darkness, which then brought light.

Matthew 25, 1 Thessalonians 3, Colossians 3:4, Psalm 57

Peace,
Phoebe

Hi Greg,

The Lord told me that the battle I am up against is the battle of the flesh; it is the leaders who are leading His church with pride and arrogance. The Lord told me that the most divisible problem in the church today is religious sectarianism. He told me that many people who are religious put their hope in religion and that many that are political put their hope in politics. Singers put their hope in singing, and so on and so forth. God is the giver of gifts, and we should lift our praises and gratitude to Him and Him alone. The Lord told me that people have to start putting their hope in Him, the one and only living Word of God.

If we want to advance in this battle we must put our hope in God and let Him fight this battle for us. We have to let His Spirit speak for us. The Lord told me that too many men allow arrogance to control their emotions, and because of this many will fail. Arrogance and pride lead to legalism. God's grace is extended to all who will receive. We are not here to judge, we are here to define and embrace a new Christianity, one that serves with humility and love. We must serve with humility because it is in humility that He brings us up. This is why we must choose to trust in our Lord with all our heart. Put the sword of pride away and take up His truth, the truth of His Word, and let us all fight the good fight of faith.

Whenever I hear someone adding a title to his or her name it really bothers me. Jesus stripped everything so that He could relate to the common folk and walk among us. He never gave Himself a worldly title, and when I hear people whom God chose to preach puff themselves up with a title it literally upsets my stomach. God gave us a name and the world gave us a title—who are we in Christ?

Another issue that bothers my spirit is when I hear people speak about who God chooses, and they walk around with a worldly measuring stick and sum up people by a worldly design. Man looks at the outward appearance but God looks at the heart. You can be whatever you want to be in this world, but that should never compete with what God has in store for you. NEVER get caught up with secularism because it builds a wall between us. Come down off the high horse and walk among us. God is love and that is what we should look like without a title.

1 Peter 1, Colossians 1-3, Psalm 23, Revelation 19

In Him,
Phoebe

Hi Greg,

Sadly, there is more discrimination within His church than I see in the world. Jesus never discriminated against anyone; He sees everyone at individual levels with potential to change in accordance with His love. We are all sinners saved by His grace – when we receive.

The whole concept to living a kingdom life is to become more like Him and continually eat from the tree of life. Jesus came to give us this Good News, but we like to conform to this world because it gives us pleasure and gratification – we like to eat from the tree of knowledge of good and evil. One leads to paradise and the other leads to debauchery, death, and destruction. We have a choice as to which tree to eat from moment by moment. When we operate from the flesh we become self-centered and destroy the paradise God gave us in the beginning. God wants us to choose to commune with Him; we have to choose to eat from the tree of life.

When Jesus came He not only tore the veil He opened the way for us to eat from the tree of life – to commune with God through Him. I still have a lot to learn, and I continually give the Lord my pride. I could choose to have so many conflicts throughout the day, but I choose to lay down my pride. Pride is the root of all divisions; greed stems from pride. I pray that I will see the day His people come together because we can accomplish more for our Lord when we work together – and that is His heart.

Mark 11, John 3:17, Psalm 34, Matthew 5, 1 Samuel 3:11

In Christ,
Phoebe

Hi Greg,

Certain Christian denominations set standards for people's lives. But what works for one family doesn't necessarily work for another. We all have to let God define the role of the family and define each individual role. Many denominations define the male and female roles based on gender. Yes, we are made differently and because of this we should work together for completeness. Let's stop trying to play God and let God do His job in each one of us. Our Lord may tell one family (e.g. Sara Grove) to go on the road and preach or sing wherever He may choose. He may tell a mother and father to leave their children and do missionary work in another country. He may tell a mother or a father to go back to school and earn a degree.

I will always support each of my children according to God's will for their life. I will not let any religion define them. God will define each one of us if we stop listening to everyone else. First we listen to God and then we listen to whomever God sends to support us in our mission. I will never forget the time I had a meeting with a pastor from a previous church, and when I told him that God was calling me to be a Christian counselor, he looked me straight in the eyes and said: "How many children do you have at home?" I responded "Five." He then told me to go back home and be a mother to my children—and here I am a messenger for His church, and it is because I put God first. God instilled a dream in my heart long ago, and here I am living it. It doesn't get any better than this.

Since that meeting long ago I vowed to listen to God first. I will not let any man define my role based on my gender. I don't want religion to define anybody's role again. We need to seek Him.

The church has fallen asleep and we are facing a war. So many times His church has bought into the lie, and I want the church to wake up to His truth. The Lord told me that our children are also Satan's target because he wants to control their mind. The mind is the battlefield, and we have an obligation to bring forth truth, not only to our minds but to our children as well. This is why we as His people have an obligation to stand up for His truth. The church of Christ has to wake up and step out of the matrix.

In a vision this morning I saw a picture of one parent with three children, and then I heard: "This is what many families look like." The Catholic Church has changed and does not excommunicate divorced couples anymore. When my parents divorced the Church condemned us. We as His body should never condemn or judge; we should support any family who is in need. I love the fact that some churches are willing to mentor children. When I chose to stay home with my children for thirteen years and provide childcare, I supported many parents who decided to work. I taught these children Christian values as it was written in my contract.

Our children are the enemy's target, and the church has to wake up to this and instill Christian values—instill His truth. If we claim to be His children then we claim to take care of each other.

My mission is John 17. The Lord wants His church to look like Him so that we can seek and save the lost. He is the Vine; we are the branches. So let's build His family, His kingdom.

Luke 8:21, Romans 1, 2 Timothy 17

Remaining in Him,
Phoebe

Hi Greg,

Jesus broke all standard cultural teaching and spoke to everyone deemed lower-class. I am to submit to our Lord before anyone else. Jesus' teaching about husbands and wives is about equality – the two shall become one – yet preachers usually don't preach on Jesus' teaching. They prefer Paul's teaching, which was culturally related. Jesus broke through all the barriers (stigmatism), and pastors are supposed to follow Jesus' example. We have to let the Lord in our lives. Submission is humility. We all need to become humble and give ourselves to the Lord and let Him teach us about truth so that He can help control the flesh.

I will submit as the Lord calls me to do so, and my husband will submit as the Lord calls him to do so. We are all here to encourage and strengthen one another in Christ, whether we are married or not. I bring my husband in on every facet of my life because I trust his input. We balance each other and need one another. We should always listen to the Word of our Lord: one man and one woman will become one.

I just witnessed a church justifying their reasoning to sin. When God reveals that a person is sinning, the best thing that person can do is repent. We all can pull scriptures out of the Bible to justify the lies we are perpetuating, and that is a sin. The Bible clearly preaches that giving is better than receiving.

Here is truth plain and simple: the more we look and act like Christ the more Christ is in us. The more we look and act like the world the more the world (flesh) is in us. We all can fall into sin, but the righteous thing to do when someone points this sin out is to confess it and repent. It is dangerous to keep on sinning because this habit will erect a wall in our relationship with God.

I previously attended a legalistic church that preached mainly on performance. I was never taught the importance of having a personal relationship with God until I read the Bible and other books regarding this. A relationship with God should be top priority. God gave me a mission, and Satan wants to thwart this mission. God gives each one of us a different mission because He did not create us the same. I first listen to God and then I listen to people He sent to support this mission. The mission will not be based on performance it will be based on my relationship with Christ.

Pastors who are bent on the peripherals in life are bent on performance. God wants a personal relationship that is not based on performance. How can anyone run His church without a personal relationship with Him? Once we choose to have a personal relationship with God, He will send His Holy Spirit to counsel us. There is so much legalism in the church today; these people set standards for all performance, and it becomes more about the performance and less about the relationship. I pray that all legalism will cease in His church, and this can be done when one ceases to listen to the flesh and commits to having a personal relationship with God.

John 9-10, John 4

In His restoring grace,
Phoebe

Hi Greg,

The Lord again gently reminded me that I can choose to use His words to build up or to tear down. He told me to use His words wisely. He also reminded me that the church is not my enemy. I have to continue to seek His wisdom because I can easily fall into a trap of deception. When I say to take a stand, it is and always will be against the schemes of the devil, not an individual or group.

As a little girl attending catechism, I remember this certain teacher who was so kind and loving. She took the time to speak to us about whom Jesus was and the significance of His love and kindness. I have never forgotten that teacher because she brought the light of Christ to me. She spoke words of truth to my heart. I may not have understood all the reasons why Jesus came, but I knew He came because He loved us. We as individuals and as a church are to be salt and light to the world, and we do this by our actions—the words will follow. How are people supposed to know the Lord unless we first imitate His love, kindness, and grace?

At my job I am never allowed to speak about Jesus unless the individual brings it up first. And once they ask, I engage in a conversation and tell them what I know. I take the same principle as Mother Teresa when she said that she couldn't help everyone, but she could help the person in front of her. If it wasn't for His church I may not have known about Christ. This catechism teacher was the first person in my life who spoke about the love of Christ, and because of this I wanted to know more about Him in my later years.

We are not here to judge and label people; we are here to be Christ to whomever we meet. I pray that His church becomes more and more like Him so that all legalism, judgment, accusation, and condemnation will cease, because then we will be free to love. I pray that His church will be Spirit-led. God created us to be dependent on Him and interdependent on each other, so let's start treating one another with love and kindness.

Luke18:1, Acts 17:30, 1 Timothy 1:2, John 8

In Christ,
Phoebe

Hi Greg,

I know God is always working in the midst of trials, and through this my relationship with Him has deepened. At one point I was very weak, and it seemed that I was getting hit from all sides. I asked Jesus how He managed to get through those tough times, and He showed me a vision of Him praying in the Garden of Gethsemane. He told me that His love is not an emotion, it is His being. He told me that if I want to have His heart I have to learn to love people even at their worst.

People talk about God's power as if it means one who is over another, but that is not the power of God. It is when one takes on a subservient role and can love even through the worst times. When a person speaks about domination, it clearly shows they are influenced by the flesh and not the love of God.

God has given me a message to help men have a different view of women, one that respects and honors women just as Jesus did. Jesus created women with a mission. What do we hear from the pulpit? We hear that women should take the submissive role and let men charge over them. We hear that it is the man's responsibility to define the woman. God told me to read 1 Timothy 2. He said that Paul was teaching Timothy the cultural demands in order to protect women. God wants to empower women with His Holy Spirit. God would not have given His Holy Spirit to women if He didn't think He could use them.

Another subject I must bring up that really bothers my spirit is money. What is being taught from the pulpit concerning money is twisted. I asked the Lord to define Malachi 3 for me. I asked Him if the storehouse represents His church. He told me that His church represents more than a building; it is His people. I pray that more pastors will preach His solid truth with His peace and love.

2 Corinthians 5

In Christ,
Phoebe

———•✦❦✦•———

Hi Greg,

Every time I choose to be obedient change happens, every time I choose to love change happens, every time I choose to be kind change happens—and every time I choose to speak His words change happens. The Lord spoke through many great people before us and change happened. Some of my favorites are Mother Teresa, Martin Luther King Jr., St. Paul, St. Stephen, Esther, and so many more. And we know that many of these great people who gave their lives to the Lord suffered. Satan silenced some these people with violence.

The Lord is so beautiful when He speaks because His words are light in this world. Jesus never condemns or accuses me. His words pierce through my heart, and when anyone buys into the lie their heart becomes poisonous. Proverbs 4:23: "Above all else, guard your heart, for it is the wellspring of life."

Always stand firm on His Word; the tempter cannot fight against this because God's truth always prevails. His message is always the same: build a relationship with Him so that you can know Him, and when you know Him and deepen the relationship, change will happen. I put my hope in Christ, not anyone else. The essence of prophecy is to give a clear witness of Jesus Christ. To distinguish between a real prophet and one who is not is by the testimony they give about Jesus.

We are not in this world to play God—we are here to live and be a witness for Christ so that the world can know Him. We need to encourage and edify one another.

John 4, Revelation 19, 1 Peter 2-3

In Christ,
Phoebe

———◦ᴆᴵᴮᴆ◦———

Hi Greg,

I had a heart-to-heart talk with our Lord. Over the past couple of weeks my heart has been changing. The Lord asked me to move out of my comfort zone. I am having a difficult time with moving from complacency. He told me there will be tribulation for my choosing this path – the path that God set before me. The world is corrupt and He needs more witnesses who will stand for His truth.

Here is truth: I tell women that God has a plan for each one of them and that His plan for them is more than they could imagine, yet I hear from women who have been indoctrinated by religion, and they think they are here to serve their husbands. I tell women that they are the daughters of the Most High God, yet I hear from men who declare from the pulpit that the woman's place is in the home. I have good news for these women: wake up and listen to God's Spirit calling you out of darkness. We are more than a title (homemaker/housewife) given to us by the world; we are the daughters of the Most High God, and that is truth.

I also speak truth about money. I couldn't care less what type of house one lives in or what clothes one wears. What I care about is when I hear pastors telling people where to give his money: The Church that God predestined is one that is united. All those who profess Jesus as their Lord and Savior have a responsibility to bring salvation to the world through Jesus Christ, His Son. If everyone who is in the family of God would invest in His Church, His Church will grow tremendously. His Church will grow through the resources that have been given from above. These resources are not limited to money; it is in our gifts, talents, and time that will enable the Body of Christ to grow. Here is truth: pray first and let God's Spirit tell the individual where to give His money. The Lord told me there are more preachers preaching His name, yet there is no depth of relationship with Him. Many start off with good intentions but then they let the world influence their heart, which can be destructive. The Lord told me that many will claim to know Him and know His voice, but that actions speak louder than words. He told me that I would know His disciples by the intentions of their heart. Pure thoughts and motivations are governed by His Spirit and not of this world.

I have a hard time giving credibility to people who look down on anyone because of the color of their skin, gender, or age. I don't give credibility to anyone poisoned by this world – especially through the media. I know His voice and I will follow Him.

One more issue that really bothers my spirit is when I hear people attaching another title to Christianity. Christianity doesn't need to have anything added to it, and if a group or organization attaches another name to it, we can know that it is inspired by the flesh. God does not separate He unites, and the demand for a title only suggests they are inspired by the world's appetites – eating from the tree of knowledge of good and evil.

John 3:6, John 6, 1 Corinthians 10:13

In Christ,
Phoebe

Hi Greg,

To be a Christian is to have a continual relationship with God. Yes, we profess our sins and claim Jesus is Lord, but there is more to being a Christian than mere words – actions must always follow. I will give the truth and be attacked for it, but that is the price I am willing to pay. When a person claims to be superior over another or spreads hate towards some group, all I can say is that you are not in a relationship with God or listening to His wisdom. God requires humility and love. Preaching about a relationship with God is truth; preaching about women being subject to men is lies. One day all this will come to an end.

Acts 11, Nehemiah 4, Philippians 1, Matthew 7, Mark 1:4, Ephesians 2

In Him always,
Phoebe

Hi Greg,

The Holy Spirit was given to us to reveal truth. Truth is given to those who have a personal relationship with our Father. God wants all to come into repentance and develop a relationship with Him. Our Father wants us to know the truth so that the truth can set us free – not to keep us in bondage. Abuse comes in various forms and control is one of them. I have counseled many Christian marriages, and I know what goes on behind closed doors. What I have learned is that women want to be loved, but how do you love a woman? You respect, value, honor, and appreciate her. Paul talks about loving the woman and respecting the man. Well, it goes both ways. I would never stay in a marriage if my husband did not love or respect me. Words are futile unless you put them into action.

John 21:18, Philippians 2:3, Acts 6

In Him,
Phoebe

Hi Greg,

An act of worship is to follow the Lord and be in obedience. A couple of months ago I asked the Lord this question: "Do You want homosexuals to be preachers?" His response was, "Let them preach for in time they will be judged just like everyone else." I asked Him about marriage and He asked me what was written in His book. I told Him one man and one woman, and He said, "Let it be." I don't know why so many preachers are preaching without a personal relationship with our Lord. The burden of proof is their teaching. The Lord told me that many preachers have a one-sided relationship with Him. Our Lord is not a forceful God; He is an all-loving God. His power of love can change a heart, and we must rely on this.

Too many people want to evangelize without the power of God's love, and it's a mistake many people make. There will be a time when the world gets so cold, and we may have to offer our lives so that many people will see the love of our Lord. We should never fear death. In fact, what I am teaching my kids now is something I never would have taught them a year ago. God has been transforming my life in such a gradual way. What I am teaching my kids is that they have the Holy Spirit, and whatever happens to their bodies is nothing compared to their spirit. I am telling them about how birth pangs may come, but the beauty that comes after is glorious. I have been using this parable so they can understand the flesh versus the spirit. A year ago I would have said that if someone were to harm any of my family members I would have taken different measures. Today I am speaking differently.

The Lord told me that He didn't die for religion; He gave His life to save our souls. When we align our souls (mind, will, and emotion) with His Spirit we then learn to live harmoniously. When we align our souls with our flesh we reap what the flesh offers – not to be confused with what the world offers. God wants us to align our everyday thinking and believing with His Spirit – this is a constant battle of the flesh. To live daily with His Spirit is when transformation will occur from within. This is why it is imperative to have a personal relationship with our Lord. Satan will do whatever he can to get our minds thinking about anything but God.

Satan has been very successful in the preaching department. To preach on issues such as having power over instead of power under is a tool the enemy has used. The mistakes preachers make is that they use our Lord for selfish endeavors. Whenever I hear anyone speak on behalf of our Lord I have to separate truth from facts. Many preachers give us facts without His truth. Here is an example I gave to my small group. The fact is that there are males and females in this world, and we are different because of our gender. The truth is that both males and females are designed by our Lord, and He died for both genders, which demonstrates nondiscrimination. The truth is that when we take that step of faith, we all are on equal grounds. Build that personal relationship with Him so that we can be more than what the world offers.

Romans 3, Colossians 2:2, 2 Corinthians 2, Romans 12

Peace,
Phoebe

Hi Greg,

Satan and his cohorts work to maintain disunity among God's people. We all are created differently, which is good, but within our differences we must put our relationship with the Lord first so we can know and appreciate those who are different within the Christian family. The churches that represent Christ look more like mercenary outposts than places of refuge. We need to set aside our differences for the love of Christ.

The Lord told me that more people are being consumed by their sins. He gave me a vision and told me that the world deceives our mind, which in turn deceives our heart, which deceives our soul, which corrupts our spirit. For those who have the Spirit of God, He inhabits the soul, which affects the heart, which affects the mind, which affects the world in a positive way. People who do not know His truth will be consumed by the lie—this is one of Satan's strategies. I was told that Satan's numbers are growing, and it is up to us (Christians) to lead people to the truth.

This morning I had a duplicate dream from the night before. In this dream a man needed some help. As I was going to help him, he held a knife to my throat, told me not to make a sound, and led me to a private area. And then the unthinkable happened. As I was being attacked by the man, I kept thinking that I had to get out of this situation. I tried to escape but he caught me and proceeded to kill me. Then I woke up from this dream. This dream served as a wake-up call so that I will not be so naive. I work in different types of settings, and some of them are questionable, so I take this dream to heart.

1 Peter 3:3, 1 Thessalonians 3:1, 1 Corinthians 5, Romans 4:16

In Him,
Phoebe

Hi Greg,

The Lord told me that our soul is the essence of our spirit. That is why it is imperative that people know our God is a God of love. Religion sucks people dry because religion claims performance. God wants us to choose Him over anything that this world can give. God gave all of us a free will, and with this free will we have a right to choose what He offers or what the world offers. Our mind signifies the belief we carry. What we believe can create a life of lies or a life of truth.

God reminded me that I am a messenger of truth. I am here to serve God in this way so that people will know His truth, and it is His truth that sets captives free. People are in bondage because they are ignorant to the truth. A person can believe and be sincere on any issue, but it doesn't necessarily reflect God's truth. I am not to judge but carry out His message. I have to give His message without any distortion. He told me that those who follow His way would listen and understand the truth, and those who do not are still in bondage.

Our Western culture is so prone to pride and greed that a darkness covers America. I have visited different cultures, and the countries I have visited don't have this heavy cloud. I know there are worse countries that carry a heavier bondage, but our culture blinds us to God's truth. Here is a question: would you be willing to give up everything – family, career, money, etc. – just to have a personal relationship with our Lord? This relationship is so vital to me that it is like breathing. I know that God has the best intentions for me, and I trust Him. I may have a lot of questions along this journey, but God likes an inquisitive mind.

Being conformed to the image of His Son takes a lot of humility. Sometimes I get so hurt when I see people abusing their authority in any religious sect. When God created the heaven and earth and all the creatures of the field, His intention was to give man responsibility to take care of His creation. As soon as Satan came on the scene it disrupted God's best intention for His creation, and soon there was "power over." When God sent His Son, Jesus, into the world, God wanted to demonstrate His love by sacrificing His Son so that in humility we would do the same. The power of this world demonstrates power over, and God's best intention is not to have power over but to serve and come under – just as Jesus did.

When anyone claims to have authority over, that person is demonstrating what the world offers. I hear these preachers preaching about God's order, and of course in their thinking their role entitles them to be on a pedestal. These people are so far from what Jesus' message is all about. Jesus used His authority to bring a different kind of order, and that is to love and serve with humility. Any other order only exists from this world. Why does God tell me to love and serve in humility? God gifted some people as preachers, teachers, and prophets so that they can send a message to everyone to have a personal relationship with Him and to be more like His Son—and that there is an eternity for all of us.

If I could only teach people one thing it would be to develop a personal relationship with our Creator. I guess you could say this is what I am doing until the day God takes me home.

3 John, Revelation 20:3, 1 Corinthians 14, Philippians 2:14

Love and peace,
Phoebe

Hi Greg,

When I first started this adventure with our Lord, I didn't have any idea what He would ask from me. I could tell you stories about my first initial experiences with the powers of darkness, but in time it will all come out. The Lord told me that I would help lead His church to victory. I asked Him how I could do this. His exact response was, "By claiming it." We all have the power in Christ to claim victory over anything.

Lately the Lord will give me a vision into people's emotion when I am standing next to them. I will see what suffering they have been through. I asked our Lord why He was giving me these visions. He told me that I could either add to it or help them through it. The Lord could provide miracles, but He wants us to choose to help and love His creation. He said that when we help people in their suffering it provides an opportunity to share in their suffering, and this provides love to that person without conditions. Our God is not a God who causes suffering, but He places Himself in people's hearts so they will know that He loves them.

We all have the ability and power to choose, and it is in this choosing that we can become more like Him. We live in a war zone, but God always claims the victory. No matter what it looks like we must choose to have an attitude of Christ. Half our battle is learning to have His attitude. In humility we gain, in pride we lose. I find life to be difficult at times, and I feel that I am always trying to keep myself afloat. As they say, "I have to take it one day at a time," and always rely on God's promises to get me through.

Psalm 19, John 10:11, Acts 1:8, Ephesians 4

In Him,
Phoebe

Hi Greg,

In a vision I had two months ago three incidents occurred. The first two lasted about a second long, and the third vision lasted three seconds. The message was quite clear. The first vision was of a man's dead body lying on the ground with his head decapitated. The second was a great explosion, and the third vision was what we need to focus on. The third vision resembled a huge concert with Jesus at the center. People of all walks of life attended, and Jesus stood at the center stage emanating this wonderful light. It was so beautiful. No matter how difficult life may get we must remember the outcome.

Our Father comes to me like a spiritual Dad, and He helps me through so many difficult times. He is like a breath of fresh air, and when I don't know what decisions to make in life, He is always leading my steps. Yes, there are times that I don't want to listen to the Lord, but when I choose not to listen to Him the result always seems to get worse. I am still learning, and I thank God that He is helping me every step of the way. The Lord is my Rock, and I pray that everyone gets to know Him on this personal level.

Too many people have a misconception about God, and I am praying that this will change. His message has been shrouded in lies, and many people need to know Him in a loving, personal way. I walk with Him and talk with Him daily. He guides and helps me no matter what the circumstance may be. Without our Lord we only exist, but with the Lord we are truly living. He brings truth in lies, love in hate, hope to the hopeless, and light in the darkness.

2 Thessalonians 3:1, 1 Peter 1:10, 1 Corinthians 15:56-57, Romans 5:2

In prayer,
Phoebe

Hi Greg,

The only security we have in this life is holding onto Christ, and I know now that it is so imperative that we teach people about the Holy Spirit – this still remains a mystery to many. It is my hope and prayer that more people will understand the Trinity. The Holy Spirit can help us through anything. The other day in communion with our Lord, He told me that He is above terrorism, He is above sexism, He is above racism, and He is above…ALL! He explained to me that whenever I focus on sexism, I start feeding into the world system. He said I need to put my faith in Him.

The other day my son Blake turned to me and said, "I know what I want to do when I grow up – I want to serve the poor." My response was, "I thought you wanted to be a pastor?" He said that he doesn't want to be a pastor because he doesn't want to take money from people. I explained where the money goes and told him about Pastor Paul of Pastor Paul's Mission. I told him that this type of pastor would be ideal for him – a community missionary pastor. This type of pastor is out among the people of the community, and they are making a difference in people's lives. I told Blake that this was my favorite type of preaching because this person helps bridge the divide, not only to those who have never heard of Christ, but to other area churches as well.

I told Blake that God never intended a church to go solo – God intended His church to work together. Whatever road God takes him on, I will encourage him to remain faithful. I teach my kids to be in prayer always and then to listen to the Holy Spirit.

It's encouraging to see that whatever life's challenges, we must hold onto the hope and faith in our Lord because He is our silver lining.

A couple of weeks ago I was feeling guilty about buying my kids Christmas gifts because I know they don't need anything, so I brought this to our Lord. Jesus told me something quite simple. He said that He looks at my heart, and He showed me a vision of myself as a little girl. He said to me, "See that little girl, she doesn't have anything to give anyone so she gives her heart." The Lord told me that I haven't changed. He said it doesn't matter if I have a little or a lot, my heart doesn't change – it is our heart that matters to God. My first love is Jesus and then my family and friends. There is nothing more precious than knowing God in an intimate way.

I don't know what the future holds in this life, but I know God is holding it – and that's comforting. My favorite Christmas song as a little girl was "The Little Drummer Boy." Now it's "Season of

Love." Every Christmas season I love to watch *A Christmas Carol* with my family – it really is about the heart.

Acts 11:28, Acts 7:55, 1 Peter 4:16, Matthew 25, 1 Peter 1:3

Reciprocal love,
Phoebe

Hi Greg,

After the previous letter the Lord spoke to me and asked, "Daughter, do you truly want to experience freedom?" My response was, "Yes!" The Lord told me that to experience freedom I must let go of my life. He told me that freedom is letting go of control. I told the Lord that if I do this, I will feel as if I am walking in this world blindfolded. His response: "Let Me be your eyes." Letting go is a difficult process. I know I listen to the Lord and comply most of the time, but not all of the time. I am a work in progress. Walking blindfolded and relying on God is the only true freedom we have in this world. Many people talk about giving up their possessions, but not many speak about giving up their life.

Another question: I wanted to know if our Lord knew every choice we make, and He told me that He knows every angle. After contemplating this answer it became apparent that our Lord knows our choices can lead to many different roads. This is why He has helped me with raising children. He could see that my choices could lead to destruction – He has interrupted certain courses of life that could have led to destruction. His Spirit is always nudging us and helping us make better choices because He knows what our choices can lead to. He tells me that although He interrupts, many people refuse to listen. I believe that most of our choices will always lead to destruction without the Lord's help because we are creatures of habit, and our habits become "us" – this could be good, bad, or ugly.

We become what we focus on. If we focus on what the world offers we become part of the world system. If we focus on Him, even though the world may crumble around us, we become like Him. We have to remember that we are not part of the world; we are in the world, but we must keep the faith no matter what the world is telling us. The Lord's truth always prevails and His Word lasts forever. Amen!

Giving up your possessions in this world or giving up your life for another is a freedom of choice. I think of it as a person going into combat. No one knows their full assignment or destiny, yet they have made the choice to sacrifice their life if need be. We don't go into combat without realizing that we may have to make the ultimate sacrifice. When we are in combat together we are at war against the enemy (Satan). God may ask us to give our life while fighting this enemy – this is how we bond and sacrifice together. Jesus Christ is our common bond, and again we need to eliminate all differences (religion, politics, etc.) and fight for the common goal.

When we make assumptions about another person's life, it can be debilitating to the kingdom. Instead of trusting in the Lord and His good works, one starts to trust in his own knowledge and understanding – I call this paralyzing. If we are in war together we should trust one another and not debilitate the work God gave. Instead of moving towards the common goal we start believing the enemy's lie and playing this tit-for-tat game. It's funny how we fall into Satan's master scheme. Focusing on the Lord, giving your life if need be, and trusting in Him is the only diversion one should take. There is no formula that outweighs God's will for our lives!

Hebrews 4:12, Job 3:19, John 5:34

He is risen,
Phoebe

All my experiences in 2010 related to one thing that I still have to master to this day: "Whatever the circumstance do what is right." In everything the Lord has taught me, His Holy Spirit is there to remind me to do what is right—if I need to forgive, I need to do so; if I need to allow grace, I need to do so; if I need to allow mercy, I need to do so; if I need to provide a meal, I need to do so; if I need to provide clothing, I need to do so...

James 2:8 (NIV) says, "If you really keep the royal law found in Scripture, 'Love your neighbor as yourself,' you are doing right." Love fulfills all Scriptures.

God bless,
Phoebe

NOTE: I started to receive a nudging from the Holy Spirit to write to the new pastor at a new church, so this is what I sent...

Hi Bill,

God has the authority over every believer. Let God operate in the hearts and minds of every believer; it is the pastor's job to initiate this.

When I awoke Saturday morning I heard this from our Lord: "Daughter of Israel, arise, for you will be sent among wolves." Who are the wolves? All I know is that wolves attack in a pack. The Lord gave me 1 John 2:15-17 (NIV): "Do not love the world or anything in the world. If anyone loves the world, love for the Father is not in them. For everything in the world—the lust of the flesh, the lust of the eyes, and the pride of life—comes not from the Father but from the world. The world and its desires pass away, but whoever does the will of God lives forever."

In Christ,
Phoebe

Hi Bill,

Last week the scene that kept coming to my mind was when Jesus told Peter who He is, and that He (Jesus) is the Rock that His church must be built upon, and the gates of hell cannot prevail against it. When Jesus spoke these words He was speaking of one church (singular). He didn't say: "Build many churches in My name." His one church represents the body of Christ, and this body of Christ is everyone who believes.

The Lord wants His children to unite in love; in doing so many will come to believe. There are so many discrepancies within His body, and many people who build up walls and call it His church are sadly mistaken. His church should be without walls, without judgment, and without rules governed by man. These manmade rules keep people away from knowing His truth. We must walk together in truth and tear down the walls and gather together to bring our God-given talents and resources so that His church will come to full fruition and He will be glorified. The gates of hell will not prevail against His church.

It would be nice to see pastors and priests alike carrying out the gospel with His full body of believers in unity instead of seeing the church divided; His church seems to be set up more like a mercenary unit. When we pool our resources together it will accomplish more than having all these churches doing life separately. Reach across the great divide and let God stir your heart accordingly. Whoever does His will is His brother, sister, and mother (Matthew 12:50).

The Lord told me that more men have a difficult time believing in Him than women, and that is why He wants to use me so that more will believe. Jesus had a difficult time with the teachers of the Law and the Pharisees because they had a hard time believing; they couldn't see with the eyes of their heart: Matthew 23. Men usually try to reason everything out, and when they cannot reason or rationalize they have a difficult time believing. Stop using your head and use your heart; you will be blessed in doing so and will experience love and joy beyond any measure that this world offers.

Whatever the Lord leads you to do just remember this thought: focus on the message and not on the messenger; too many people get caught up with the peripheral. We are all sinners desperately needing a Savior. No one is greater than the other for we are all on the same team; we are all in the same boat. We need to encourage and edify one another so that we can advance His kingdom. Whenever I move forward I don't see any obstacles, I focus on the love I have for our Lord, and this alone motivates me to do anything. The Lord can use me any way He wants. God created everything and everyone for His majesty and glory; we give God pleasure when we glorify Him by doing His will.

Exodus 34

In His love and mercy,
Phoebe

Hi Bill,

May the grace and peace of our Lord Jesus Christ be with you.

I received this message last Friday, and I pray that the words from our Lord do not fall on deaf ears. Mark 4:9: "Let those who have ears listen and understand."

The sum of all parts equals the whole. Each Christian church represents the whole body of Christ – Jesus is the Head. God has a simple message with a simple answer: Jesus Christ! He is the way, the truth, and the life. But what do people do with this simple message of hope? They dilute and distort it with the power of the world. We have a sincere obligation to give truth to people and that truth is Jesus Christ. People do not need to add to this truth. Jesus came to save us from our sins and to release freedom in those who believe. John 3:16-17 (NIV): "For God so loved the world that He gave His one and only Son, that whoever believes in Him shall not perish but have eternal life. For God did not send His Son to condemn the world, but to save the world through Him."

Many people from various denominations have distorted this simple truth; many people believe that performance supersedes this simple message. Performance does not supersede John 3:16-17. Sometimes when I enter a Christian church I hear this from the pulpit: one must be baptized in order to go to heaven…one must speak in tongues in order to have the Holy Spirit…one must tithe in order to be blessed from God…one must speak a certain way in order to have the Holy Spirit…one must come under the pope because he has the answers…blah, blah, blah. God wants everyone to hear and understand that Jesus Christ and only Jesus Christ is the answer. Nothing should be added or taken away from this simple truth. Believing in Jesus Christ is our hope for a lost world. And those who have believed and taken Jesus Christ into their hearts will be saved.

But this is not the finish. Those who have taken Jesus into their hearts will have the Holy Spirit in them to do God's will. Each individual is equipped with gift(s) from the Spirit of God to carry out God's plan. When we believe in Jesus Christ and take Him into our heart it is just the beginning of something new that God has in store for us. Our goal is to become the best that we can be in Christ; we all are different with different gifts from God. We all can learn from our Lord Jesus Christ, the perfect example, but we must know the truth—that God created us with different qualities.

Each believer has the Spirit of God within them to carry out His purpose and plan. Jesus said that we can do more than He did. John 14:12-14 (NIV): "Very truly I tell you, whoever believes in me will do the works I have been doing, and they will do even greater things than these, because I am going to the Father. And I will do whatever you ask in my name, so that the Father may be glorified in the Son. You may ask for anything in my name and I will do it."

According to His will and purpose, God is asking each believer to rise up with his or her unique qualities and do His will in order to carry out His plan. We can work together individually and collectively as this is God's plan. He wants His believers to be interconnected because when we are one He is glorified. God has the right to be the author of each believer; He created each one of us uniquely, so within these differences let's learn to accept and appreciate God's purpose for each believer.

Please allow grace to overflow for yourself and for others. Here is what God wants from each believer: believe in Him; believe that He sent His Son to save us from our sins; believe that each person in the Bible is unique and God used each one according to his or her character. Believe that God can and will use each believer's gifts and unique character to carry out His will on earth as it is in heaven. Jesus is the hope of the world and His Spirit lives within each believer; we must also be the hope for the world.

I had a vision the other night. When I closed my eyes to sleep I saw a person in full armor riding on a warhorse and traveling very fast through heaven. As this warrior was traveling I saw the stars move out of his way. This warrior was holding up a banner that had TRUTH written across it. And then I heard: "Gird yourself with TRUTH!" I saw many different types of angels and noticed one very tall and strong angel. And then Ephesians 6:10-17 came to mind.

In Him,
Phoebe

Hi Bill,

The other day as I was pondering the vision I shared regarding "TRUTH," I remember feeling love, happiness, excitement, and joy, but when I saw this one strong tall angel who stood out among the others, I felt very concerned. This angel did not make a move; he just stared and seemed very calculating.

I asked God to always keep me humble, and every time I send a message of God's hope and truth I am bombarded with doubt from the enemy. This doubt only confirms that I am doing something significant for our Lord. I always put the doubts to rest with His truth. I believe that when the Lord uses someone for His will and purpose it furthers His kingdom. God wants all of us to walk humbly with Him. In pride one becomes cynical, legalistic, judgmental, and complaining; in humility one has an appreciation for God and everything He created—one trusts and relies on Him.

Now I would like to share another vision I had last week. While I was cleaning my house I experienced a strange vision out of the blue, and in this vision I saw multiple demons tearing and gnawing at my flesh until my body was torn to shreds. The only response I had was "BIG DEAL, at least I know where I am going." And then I moved on. I do NOT feed into fear or deception! Anyone who has chosen Jesus as his or her Lord and Savior has to understand something significant: we are more than flesh. In Christ, we also have His Spirit who is able to defeat any adversary. And we can obviously do this (with His power) together in unity with one body and one Spirit (Ephesians 4:1-6)!

A couple of weeks ago when I was trying to sleep the Lord gave me a vision I will NEVER forget. I have this strong faith in God, and no one can take this away from me, but the Lord reminded me of where I was spiritually when I first started on a quest for His truth. He took me back to when I first started getting dreams and visions and how I felt so confused, and in this confusion I was very insecure, scared, and full of doubt. And as the Lord took me back to that place of doubt and confusion He said: "Do not put new wine into old wineskins."

I didn't understand what God was doing so I asked my pastor about it. He assured me that God does not talk to any of us (currently) through dreams and visions, only through His Written Word, the Bible. He also assured me that God wants women to be subjected to their husband's authority. I remember being so confused, ignorant, and naive about God and His Word, but as my desire grew for His truth, the more I would read the Bible and receive messages, dreams, and visions.

I kept searching for anyone who could affirm what was happening to me. I can't tell you how many tears I have shed due to male preachers discriminating against me because of my gender. Finally, when I asked my seminary professor and pastor (Greg Boyd) if God can speak to women through dreams and visions, he said "of course" and gave me passages to validate this. This was the first time I felt validated by a pastor. So you see, I had my struggles, but in the immense emotional pain I could always feel God's love for me; today my faith is stronger than ever. I have fought many battles to have a beautiful relationship with our Lord God, and it's all worth it.

In His truth,
Phoebe

Hi Bill,

I am apprehensive about sending this message, but if I were to ignore it His blood would be on me. Whenever and however the Holy Spirit wants to work in each heart let it be. The Lord is very specific with this message. He told me: "My church has become licentious." When I responded that I didn't understand, the Lord told me that the leaders of His church would know exactly what this means.

The Lord is indignant about this message. He is trying to reach the lost, and His church was built for this purpose. Those who receive these messages that I send but do not heed the warnings are not with God. Either a person is for God or against Him – either a person serves God or doesn't, so choose and choose wisely. I asked the Lord how one knows if the church leaders are for or against Him and He answered: "Those who love Me will do My Father's will." I asked the Lord what would happen to those leaders in His church who continually lead people astray by their pride and arrogance. The Lord said if they don't repent and do His will they will be without a shepherd. The Lord wants many to come to Him and repent and ask for forgiveness, and by His mercy and grace they are forgiven.

In Genesis 4:6, the Lord explained to me how He gave Cain a chance to turn things around and "do what is right," but because of Cain's pride and jealousy the sin took him away from God's blessing: "Then the Lord said to Cain, 'Why are you angry? Why is your face downcast? If you do what is right, will you not be accepted? But if you do not do what is right, sin is crouching at your door; it desires to have you, but you must rule over it.'"

God wanted Cain to master the sin in his life so that he could commune with God, but Cain chose otherwise. I always remind myself and others how to deal with the repetitive sin in life: don't let your brain take you where you don't want to go; everything starts with a thought. We need to remind ourselves that the Holy Spirit is always there to help us with any temptations in our lives. If our Lord prayed for His apostles and all of humanity not to be seduced by sin, we should realize we need help with this and not be ignorant of how sin can rule over us if we choose to let it. We all have a choice to master the sin in our life by the power of the Holy Spirit. Jesus' blood was shed for our sins, but sin is still pervasive and part of our nature.

God is for us and gave us a way to overcome the sins that keep us from being spiritually mature. Spiritual maturity simply means that we do what is right in His sight – we all know right from wrong, and we just have to put off the old way of doing life, the old way of thinking. What I have learned is that true life is communing with our Lord moment by moment. Forgiveness equals restoration, and Christ wants relationships restored; love and forgiveness are at the core of a healthy relationship. Our Lord died for our sins so that we can commune and have a relationship with Him, and then teach this to others. He makes all things new. Bury the past and be a new creation in Christ.

Satan is a deceiver. Do not partake in evil as this takes your heart away from the Lord, and you cannot serve two masters. I asked this question of our Lord: "Is each soul who professes faith in You always saved?" His response: "Wherever your heart is, is where your soul will take you." Here is a simple truth from our Lord: "Never partake in evil; serve Me only. I died for love and for the forgiveness of sin, now use them both. Whatever sin takes you from Me, profess the sin, repent, and forgive, and I will wipe away the stains and make everything new. My grace is sufficient, but in order for a person to keep serving Me he has to continue serving me. Whatever is true is real, and I tell you this because Satan desires to have you, and Satan will take whatever I give and deceive many. Know the truth as this will set you free from the bondage of sin; break those chains and be a new creation in Me."

God promises that if He is for us who can be against us? What I do know is that how we live on earth and who we serve matters to our Lord: Jesus holds the keys to heaven and hell (Revelation 1:18). God is love by showing us His mercy, grace, and forgiveness, and if a person doesn't know this in his heart he really doesn't know the Lord's heart.

This world is never about us, it's about leading people to the Lord. That is why the Lord has stricter adherences for His leaders because He wants each leader to be preaching about Him. A good leader leads people to Christ and also makes great leaders. There are so many Pauline pastors who glorify Paul more than Jesus, but never forget what Jesus did for Paul – He saved him. God used Paul for his strength and He also used him for his weakness in order to humble him – but God! The Lord will use each one of us according to His will and purposes. Paul was a living testimony and example of living out this faith.

I asked our Lord what He wants from each one of us and He said that He wants our heart. He wants us to freely choose love, and in this love we will find Him. Jesus is our treasure, and whenever we choose to listen and obey His Holy Spirit the treasure that we store up in heaven is love. It is our love for Him that makes us love others and build His kingdom – His kingdom is His people.

I wouldn't want to hear a message from a preacher who claims to be a cessationist because most of his messages would forget Jesus and fall into pride: "Pride goeth before a fall." (If you want to test a person's character give them power.) I need to ask: What need is there for the Holy Spirit if you think some of these gifts have ceased? Ephesians 4:11 says that Jesus gives the gifts accordingly, and "all will cease when the perfect comes." In 1 Corinthians 13:10 it is understood that all will be perfect (complete) when He comes back – there will be no more building His kingdom when we are with Him in glory!

The difference between the Old Testament and the New Testament is that the Holy Spirit indwells those who profess Jesus is Lord, and the Lord gives His gifts accordingly to build His kingdom. When a person freely receives Christ he should freely pass this information on. Whatever blessings we freely receive from our Lord we are blessed to freely give. Remember, all those who wrote the New Testament knew the Old Testament very well and quoted from it under the inspiration of the Holy Spirit. When leaders of His current church bring forth information from the OT to the NT, I would hope they make sure it has nothing to do with legalism or performance; Jesus didn't die for this purpose.

When Jesus was carrying His cross He said He was making everything new. Yes, our Lord doesn't change (immutable) but people do, and that is exactly what God wants – to make us a new creation in Christ. For God's sake let's build His kingdom in unity instead of letting our pride and arrogance tear it down. The veil was torn for all to come before our Lord, so get rid of the malice, division, and strife being displayed in His current church – for our Lord's sake.

The Lord wants an army of believers who will fight the good fight of faith: choose your side and do not have one foot in and one foot out; our Lord wants those who are committed. He is coming for His bride, washed clean from any stain, wrinkle, or blemish.

Revelation 3, Hebrews 4:12, Philippians 2:4

In Him,
Phoebe

Hi Bill,

May God bless you and everyone you touch with all the works that you do for Him.

The words of knowledge I kept getting these past weeks: "People will perish for not knowing His truth." Scriptures for meditation are John 14 and Revelation 2.

When I read John 14, verses 30-31 (NIV) come off the pages very strongly: "I will not say much more to you, for the prince of this world is coming. He has no hold over me, but he comes so that the world may learn that I love the Father and do exactly what my Father has commanded me."

John 17 is my passion and mission, and people are perishing every day because they do not know the Lord, but John 14:30-31 reflects John 17, which reflects the love of God. Many people have a hole in their heart, and they try to fill this void with the fruit of the flesh: lust, greed, pride, lies, self-ambition, disorder, disobedience, hate, and dissention, etc. What the world offers is antithetical to God. God wants us to trust and believe in Him and trust and believe His Word and promises. God offers us hope and an everlasting life with Him, and this world offers fleshly desires that only please the flesh.

We need to daily crucify our flesh in order to create unity—for God. We glorify Him when we are unified. Nothing pleases God more than when we work together in unity and harmony. This can only happen when we act on this belief; on the belief that Jesus wants unity because when we do so it takes on an energy force in the spiritual realm that God blesses (Satan notices this as well). When we believe in our Father, His Spirit through Jesus Christ guides us into all truth, and when we act on this truth we are utilizing the Holy Spirit.

I was explaining this truth to my youngest daughter. I wanted Brooke to know that we all have a choice to operate in the flesh or initiate the Holy Spirit to operate in truth. We need to call on the Holy Spirit daily because it is so easy to fall back into our old habits. When we take a step towards God with our daily choices He responds to those choices. He has our best intentions in mind. God does NOT want perfect people; God wants a heart that lives for Him so we can express this towards His creation.

Whenever we speak by faith, confidence, and expectancy, we can know that God is operating in the spiritual realm for our good. God loves us so much that He gave us free will, and by loving us unconditionally He lets us decide to choose Him or reject Him. And once we choose God and what He did on the cross for us we daily die to the self and intentionally live for Christ moment by moment. Jesus' life on earth is a testimony to this. I continually have to rely on God because I can so easily be persuaded by the world.

God's mission for His people is not in the building, it's all over the world. The church is a place to hear God's truth so that we can profess Jesus as our Lord and Savior, know who we are in Christ, and have a personal relationship with Him. We need to operate by the works of the Spirit so that we can do the same work in the world that Jesus did. Every time I read Revelation 2, it reflects Jesus' teachings about continuing His work and pressing on until unity is on the hearts of His people. When people who do not know Christ see this unified love among God's people, more will come to know Him.

There is a world out there that needs to hear about the Lord, and it is in our own back yard – the mission field is everywhere we are present because God is in us. Everything starts with prayer. Hosea 3:4-5 (NIV): "For the Israelites will live many days without king or prince, without sacrifice or sacred stones, without ephod or household gods. Afterward the Israelites will return and seek the Lord their God and David their king. They will come trembling to the Lord and to his blessings in the last days."

Every time we move towards God with our unconditional love He responds with His unconditional love. It's like a beautiful harmonious dance.

Believing in Him,
Phoebe

Hi Bill,

God is love and Jesus is the heart of God manifested in flesh. We are all in a spiritual battle, especially those who confess Jesus as their Lord and Savior. We can be deceived and backslide with our daily sins if we are not aware of this. What I see happening is that many people who profess Jesus as their Lord and Savior are still being deceived. It is not like buying life insurance. It is about the heart, which is why Jesus came to show the world that He is love and that He devised a plan for all of us to know, love, and believe in Him. God wants no one to perish, but many are being deceived and many reject Him because they don't really know the truth—the enemy continually distorts the truth.

The enemy wants to kill, steal, and destroy God's creation, and he comes "like a lion" seeking whom he can devour. Notice that phrase "like a lion"; the enemy is a counterfeit to everything that is true, beautiful, lovely, and pure (Jesus). He wants to destroy God's creation by distorting God's truth. The truth is that Jesus is the Lion of Judah (Revelation 5:5). The enemy tries to poison everything God made for His glory, and that is why God cast him out of heaven and into the pit of hell. Hell was designed for Satan and his cohorts, not for God's creation on earth. Jesus warns us about hell many times, and He does this because He loves us and wants His creation to be aware of this.

I have a friend who was a professing Christian and got baptized in her early years, but in her twenties she started doing her own thing and rejecting God. She mocked Christians and basically told God she didn't need Him in her life, so she started enjoying her sin – she didn't love God anymore. She was very mean to whoever came across her path until one day she had a major car accident and was in a coma for three months.

She told me that right before she woke up from the coma demons were tormenting her, and she could smell a putrid stench like burning flesh. The screams from the pit below were so horrifying that the screams alone scared her. She told me the demons were trying to push her into this pit, and when she yelled "Jesus Christ!" at that very moment she woke up from her three-month coma.

I asked her about the seal from the Holy Spirit, and she told me that she broke the seal – she wanted nothing to do with God. After this experience she turned her heart back to God. It is by the power of Jesus that we are saved by His grace, but we should not be ignorant of the enemy's schemes: 2 Corinthians 2:11. As Jesus told me, "wherever your heart is, is where your soul will take you." People can believe or not believe in this story, but I base everything on the Word of God. The Word of God is truth, and God wants us to believe in His Word. God gave us the power in Jesus' name to cast out any demonic forces, and we have the right to do that, but we have to believe in Him – He has to live in our heart.

A friend came over and wanted to talk with me because she was going through a lot and wanted to vent. I listened without judgment as her words kept flowing from her heart. She told me that she cried all night, and as she was crying out to God she told Him about the terrible choices she had made and how these choices almost cost her life. She loves the Lord but she loves her sin as well. I told her to start afresh and nail her sins to the cross, and I reminded her that God forgives our sins when we lay them at His feet. I told her to let go of the guilt and condemnation and look forward to a new day as she starts making better decisions. I asked God to help her with her daily walk as He is there for her.

This reminded me of how I used to view my owns sins: I made a terrible decision a long time ago, and this decision kept me from going to church because I felt that I could never be forgiven. I had an abortion. I was raised and baptized in the Catholic faith, but I never really had a personal relationship with our Lord as I do now. I thank God that He has forgiven and redeemed me and made me new. I am finding out how many women struggle with the same guilt/sin, but God nailed that sin to the cross.

Missing the mark makes us ALL dependent on Jesus. God loves me, and because I can lay my sins at the cross daily I can actually like myself. What I am learning is that when I like myself it is easy to love others – it really is! This has nothing to do with performance; it has everything to do with my daily walk with the Lord. I thank God for His mercy, grace, love, and forgiveness.

Visions: I saw a bride who was in a skeletal form burning, and then I saw a beautiful radiant bride glowing. I asked the Lord what this meant, and He told me that for everything that is real and true there will always be a counterfeit – "be aware and don't let your heart be troubled for I am with you." I saw a cloud open up and angels ascending and descending from heaven; one was HUGE and carrying a golden sword as he descended.

Proverbs 4:23 (NIV): "Above all else, guard your heart, for everything you do flows from it." For wherever your heart is your soul will take you (Matthew 6:19-21). The treasure of God is His kingdom; seek Him and all His righteousness first!

Exodus 19:5, John 4:14, 1 Thessalonians 2:14, Mark 12:33, Psalm 33

In Him,
Phoebe

I wrote the above July 10, and since then the Lord has spoken to me many times. He said that as we are building His kingdom Satan is building his as well. The Lord told me that Satan is devouring the flesh of those who turn from Him. We live in a world where this is easily possible because humans are subjected to the lie every day. I was walking to work early one morning when I came across a very young beautiful woman, and as I walked by her a demon came out of her and hissed at me. I am not imagining this; the Lord wants to show us that Satan possesses more and more people.

The Lord told me that Satan will use people to come against Him, and these people will create a divergence to Him by creating a form of allegiance with their knowledge and power. We are to resist this temptation as it is not from God. I never wanted to write this because those who are not in Christ will not understand. But the Lord told me that He is going to reveal more to me so that

I can understand His truth. He also said that I will become best friends to those who are in Christ, but to those who are not in Christ I will become their worst enemy. His ways are higher than our ways, and we must never look to the left or right, but always look to Him for answers.

The Lord reminds me to stay on the path that is most resisted, which leads to suffering, but He told me that I will be with Him in His glory one day. He reminds me not to lean on my own understanding but depend on Him and He will make my path straight. Mightier is He who is in us than he who is in the world. One thing that is increasing in me is this confidence I have in the Lord; this trust consumes me like a fire. People will perish for lack of knowledge of the truth!

Proverbs 3, 1 John 4, Luke 16

In Christ,
Phoebe

Hi Bill,

The enemy certainly knows God's beauty and creation, and whenever His truth is revealed the enemy comes around to destroy or distort His truth. I am writing this book to help people understand our Father God, His Son Jesus Christ, and His helper, the Holy Spirit. All books that have been written, all books that are being written, and all books that will be written should point to the Bible. The Bible, whether it is the Old Testament or the New Testament, is always pointing to Jesus Christ. If any book dissuades you from knowing who Jesus (truth) is then get rid of it. I personally love to read, and I hope this book will help people on their journey with our Lord.

My path is not for everyone, but God has called me out to awaken His church. He wants His church to have a deeper, more intimate relationship with Him so that we all can grow in our trust in Him. God wants a revival in His church and all this means is that God wants His children's hearts revived for Him. John 17 burns within me, and I will not stop speaking about unity within His church until the Lord comes back.

Now, the Lord reminded me how to forgive someone. The Lord told me that when I forgive someone's transgressions, I am partaking in His suffering. Every time we forgive someone we are taking on their sins as Jesus did on the cross, and it doesn't stop there. The Lord said that when we partake in this suffering we need to cast the burden on Him so we don't get weighed down.

I know this too well. A long time ago after I was forcefully attacked I forgave this person right afterwards, and it seemed to release something from him because he started to cry—a burden lifted from him. But soon after this attack and forgiving him, I started going into a deep depression until things spiraled out of control. I developed an eating disorder and my whole outlook on security changed; my trust for people and God changed. I felt like a loser. On the outside I acted as if everything were the same, but I kept it all to myself and did not release anything to anyone.

This is why it is imperative to release forgiveness to God and give this burden to Him. He will lift it from us and nail it to the cross so that we will not get weighed down; He will set us free. When I forgive in this way, the burden is lifted from me and peace overwhelms my soul. It enables me to move on and not get stuck.

For the love of God, let's put away the selfish attitude and get rid of anything that prevents us from building His kingdom. Keep your eyes fixed on Jesus and your eyes will be opened. All those who have Jesus in their heart have the authority to cast out anything that is not of Him. We have that authority, but some of us are blind to this or we forget – never forget who you are in Christ and what He has done for you!

Whether we are in the "end times" or not, just remember something about our Lord: He is victorious. It may look like we are losing the battle, but just remember who wins the war! Amen to that!

A couple of weeks ago I was with my family at our cabin and I was reading through Matthew. When I set the Bible down the pages turned back to Daniel 12. As I was reading through Daniel 12 two passages stood out—they almost lifted from the page: Daniel 12:3 and 12:10.

Daniel 12:3 (NIV): "Those who are wise will shine like the brightness of the heavens, and those who lead many to righteousness, like the stars for ever and ever."

Daniel 12:10 (NIV): "Many will be purified, made spotless and refined, but the wicked will continue to be wicked. None of the wicked will understand, but those who are wise will understand."

2 Corinthians 1:9, 1 Timothy 6, Revelation 19

In His love,
Phoebe

Hi Bill,

In 2000 during a trip to Ireland I was standing on the edge of the Cliff of Moher looking down at God's majesty when out of the blue I heard: "Jump, go ahead, you want to be with Him so badly – just jump; it will only take a second and you'll be with Him." And as I heard this I removed myself from the edge and said, "You're not worth it."

We have to know the enemy and his schemes and not let his lies come into our heart. When we know Jesus we can discern; Jesus said His sheep will hear His voice – we will know that good comes from above and any act of evil is the work of Satan. Jesus is our daily manna (His Word), and when we walk in the Spirit we can let go of our strongholds in this world and give everything to God. God wants us to know Him on an intimate level through His Son, Jesus Christ. Please take time to know who you are in Christ as it will change your life.

Colossians 2:20 (NIV): "Since you died with Christ to the elemental spiritual forces of this world, why, as though you still belonged to the world, do you submit to its rules: Satan is the ruler of the world…But Jesus is the head over all rule and authority."

Corinthians 3:17 (NIV): "Now the Lord is the Spirit, and where the Spirit of the Lord is, there is freedom."

The responsibility of binding and loosing falls upon us; we are God's messengers of a gospel that can deliver and set people free.

The Lord's Prayer

Matthew 6:9-13 (NIV):

Our Father in heaven,
hallowed be your name,
your kingdom come,
your will be done,
on earth as it is in heaven.
Give us today our daily bread.
And forgive us our debts,
as we also have forgiven our debtors.
And lead us not into temptation,
but deliver us from the evil one.

There is a spiritual war going on, and many people are oblivious to this. Every day I see with spiritual eyes the agony and suffering people are going through without the defense of knowing who they are in Christ. I want those who are "Christ ones" to rise up and be the people God created them to be. We are His children, and we need to stand up and fight back with His Spirit and help those who do not know the Lord understand who they are in Christ and what God has done for them. I want people to understand that God LOVES US and wants the best for us, and I want people to know who God is.

The Lord is a beautiful, loving God who wants no one to perish and wants to empower us to stand against the schemes of Satan. I want everyone to know that the power comes from within and that God is working for us and not against us. Let go of the title, age, color, gender, or status, and let go of anything that was given to you from this world. Give yourself a new name and that is: Child of God!

I want this book to empower people with the power of God. I will NOT sit back and watch another person die without knowing who their Creator is. Jesus gave us authority by the power of the Holy Spirit to overcome the snares of the enemy. Jesus wants us to have freedom in Him.

Luke 4:14-21 (NIV):

Jesus returned to Galilee in the power of the Spirit, and news about him spread through the whole countryside. He was teaching in their synagogues, and everyone praised him. He went to Nazareth, where he had been brought up, and on the Sabbath day he went into the synagogue, as was his custom. He stood up to read, and the scroll of the prophet Isaiah was handed to him. Unrolling it, he found the place where it is written: "The Spirit of the Lord is on me, because he has anointed me to proclaim good news to the poor. He has sent me to proclaim freedom for the prisoners and recovery of sight for the blind, to set the oppressed free, to proclaim the year of the Lord's favor." Then he rolled up the scroll, gave it back to the attendant and sat down. The eyes of everyone in the synagogue were fastened on him. He began by saying to them, "Today this scripture is fulfilled in your hearing."

Matthew 28:18 (NIV): "Then Jesus came to them and said, 'All authority in heaven and on earth has been given to me.'"

Matthew 28:18 (NIV) "Jesus called his twelve disciples to him and gave them authority to drive out impure spirits and to heal every disease and sickness."

Luke 10:19 (NIV): "I have given you authority to trample on snakes and scorpions and to overcome all the power of the enemy; nothing will harm you."

Spiritual warfare is for the purpose of setting the captives free; it involves using the keys of the kingdom: "I will give you the keys of the kingdom of heaven; whatever you bind on earth will be bound in heaven, and whatever you loose on earth will be loosed in heaven" (Matthew 16:19 NIV). As we pray the Word in the name of Jesus, the Holy Spirit's anointing and power will unlock the minds of the captives so that the gospel of Christ will set them free. Realize that Jesus wants you to be free!

John 8:32 (NIV): "Then you will know the truth, and the truth will set you free."

Before Jesus' ascension He loosened those whom Satan had bound. Jesus has given His authority (in His name) to us to carry this out. He supplied everything to set us free.

Galatians 3:13 (NIV): "Christ redeemed us from the curse of the law by becoming a curse for us, for it is written: 'Cursed is everyone who is hung on a pole.'" Our Lord wants us to believe in Him and believe in His promises.

John 15:26 (NIV): "When the Advocate comes, whom I will send to you from the Father—the Spirit of truth who goes out from the Father—he will testify about me."

Ephesians 6:10-18 (NIV):

Finally, be strong in the Lord and in his mighty power. Put on the full armor of God, so that you can take your stand against the devil's schemes. For our struggle is not against flesh and blood, but against the rulers, against the authorities, against the powers of this dark world and against the spiritual forces of evil in the heavenly realms. Therefore put on the full armor of God, so that when the day of evil comes, you may be able to stand your ground, and after you have done everything, to stand. Stand firm then, with the belt of truth buckled around your waist, with the breastplate of righteousness in place, and with your feet fitted with the readiness that comes from the gospel of peace. In addition to all this, take up the shield of faith, with which you can extinguish all the flaming arrows of the evil one. Take the helmet of salvation and the sword of the Spirit, which is the word of God. And pray in the Spirit on all occasions with all kinds of prayers and requests. With this in mind, be alert and always keep on praying for all the Lord's children.

If you want to know the heart of our God, read John 17 (NIV):

After Jesus said this, he looked toward heaven and prayed: 'Father, the hour has come. Glorify your Son, that your Son may glorify you. For you granted him authority over all people that he might give eternal life to all those you have given him. Now this is eternal life: that they know you, the only true God, and Jesus Christ, whom you have sent. I have brought you glory on earth by finishing the work you gave me to do. And now, Father, glorify me in your presence with the glory I had with you before the world began. I have revealed you to those whom you gave me out of the world. They were yours; you gave them to me and they have obeyed your word. Now they know that everything you have given me comes from you. For I gave them the words you gave me and they accepted them. They knew with certainty that I came from you, and they believed that you sent me. I pray for them. I am not praying for the world, but for those you have given me, for they are yours. All I have is yours, and all you have is mine. And glory has come to me through them. I will remain in the world no longer, but they are still in the world, and I am coming to you. Holy Father, protect them by the power of your name, the name you gave me, so that they may be one as we are one. While I was with them, I protected them and kept them safe by that name you gave me. None has been lost except the one doomed to destruction so that Scripture would be fulfilled. I am coming to you now, but I say these things while I am still in the world, so that they may have the full measure of my joy within them. I have given them your word and the world has hated them, for they are not of the world any more than I am of the world. My prayer is not that you take them out of the world but that you protect them from the evil one. They are not of the world, even as I am not of it. Sanctify them by the truth; your word is truth. As you sent me into the world, I have sent them into the world. For them I sanctify myself, that they too may be truly sanctified. My prayer is not for them alone. I pray also for those who will believe in me through their message, that all of them may be one, Father, just as you are in me and I am in you. May they also be in us so that the world may believe that you have sent me. I have given them the glory that you gave me, that they may be one as we are one—I in them and you in me—so that they may be brought to complete unity. Then the world will know that you sent me and have loved them even as you have loved me. Father, I want those you have given me to be with me where I am, and to see my glory, the glory you have given me because you loved me before the creation of the world. Righteous Father, though the world does not know you, I know you, and they know that you have sent me. I have made you known to them, and will continue to make you known in order that the love you have for me may be in them and that I myself may be in them.

In Him,
Phoebe

JESUS...

In chemistry, He turned water to wine.

In biology, He was born without the normal conception.

In physics, He disproved the law of gravity when He ascended into heaven.

In economics, He disproved the law of diminishing returns by feeding five thousand men with two fishes and five loaves of bread.

In medicine, He cured the sick and the blind without administering a single dose of drugs.

In history, He is the beginning and the end.

In government, He said that He shall be called Wonderful Counselor, Prince of Peace.

In religion, He said no one comes to the Father except through Him.

Jesus had no servants, yet they called Him Master; had no degree, yet they called Him Teacher; had no medicines, yet they called Him Healer.

He had no armies, yet rulers feared Him.

He won no military battles, yet He conquered the world.

He committed no crime, yet they crucified Him.

He was buried in a tomb, yet He lives today.

I feel honored to serve such a leader who loves us! Join us and let's celebrate Him; He is worthy.

The eyes beholding this message shall not behold evil, the hand that sends this message forward shall not labor in vain, and the mouth that says "amen" to this prayer shall smile forever.

Grace, peace, and mercy to all who read this book. He is our Shepherd who is ever leading us.

Epilogue

After compiling my journals I felt it was time to have it published. Psalm 68:11(NIV): "The Lord gave some a word; great was the company of those that published it." I know the Lord is nudging my heart to do this because who knows when our time is up or when the earth will fade away? I hope and pray that this book will open some reader's mind to the truth. The words you've read in these pages records my own profound experience with the Trinity, and it is my hope that the reader will come away with a better understanding of God's character: God as the Father, God as the Son, and God as the Holy Spirit.

Please get to know God so you too can experience Him in this most profound, beautiful, and personal way. Everyone's experience with God will be their own, and I am hoping that a personal relationship with our Father will blossom with each reader. It doesn't matter what you did in the past; Jesus is standing at the door knocking and waiting for you to receive Him. God is the only author of His book, and He is true to His promises: "seek and you will find."

God has helped me in so many ways on my quest for the truth, and I am glad that I documented His truth in a book so that many can learn and appreciate His true character. There may be skeptics regarding this book, but that is none of my concern; my identity is in Christ, not in anyone else. We are all different, and therefore we are going to think differently, but if we keep Jesus at the center and humble ourselves daily, pride cannot consume us to condemn others. We are here to show love, mercy, grace, and forgiveness to others and to ourselves.

My heart is to serve the Lord, and my experiences with our Lord are daily as I have learned to trust and walk with Him – I hope everyone will do the same. Jesus is alive and active, and it is my prayer that His church will keep building on this. It is my heart and prayer that many people will come to know our Lord on a personal basis, turn their heart to Him, and profess Jesus as their Lord and Savior. Here is a simple prayer of salvation.

Prayer for Salvation:

Heavenly Father, in Jesus' name I repent of my sins and open my heart to let Jesus come inside of me. Jesus, You are my Lord and Savior. I believe You died for my sins and were raised from the dead. Fill me with Your Holy Spirit. Thank You, Father, for saving me in Jesus' name. Amen.

God loves us all, and sin separated us from God. Jesus died for our sins so that we can know God's love for us. God went to great lengths to save us. God loves you; believe and receive Him!

Reflection

I dedicate this book to all those who have lost hope in this world. There is a spiritual war going on around us, and God wants each one of us to know His truth. In truth, there is one God who can eradicate the poison/lies that are being administered in this world and His name is Jesus Christ/Word of God. We are all in a spiritual battle and when we know who we are in Christ our life takes on a new identity. When we renew our mind every day to God's truth we can stand against any schemes of the one who comes "like a lion." Satan' wants to kill, steal and destroy God's Creation and God wants us to resist him and we can do this in a very powerful way when we know who we are in Christ. God is calling His children to work together with Him and for Him. There is power in numbers and in His blood, and knowing this we can gain confidence and be empowered by the Holy Spirit to do is His will, but we must do this together. It is time for the Body of Christ to rise and come together and be empowered with His Holy Spirit!

We can trust in God's promises and know that the battle we are fighting is His. In truth, the battle we are fighting is already won and Christ is victorious! (Revelation 19:11-21)